SPURS TO CREATIVE THINKING

By R.E. Myers, Ed.D.

Pieces of Learning

© 2002 Pieces of Learning
www.piecesoflearning.com
CLC0274
ISBN 1-931334-10-2
Printed in the U.S.A.

WHO NEEDS THIS BOOK?

SPURS TO CREATIVE THINKING in Language Arts was conceived primarily to show how Torrance's 18 creative thinking skills can inspire the language arts curriculum and how they can encourage students to think productively. (See Torrance, E. P. and H. T. Safter, The Incubation Model of Teaching, 1990.) Accordingly, any teacher who is involved with the language arts – and what teacher isn't? – will find it eye-opening. For example, if we consider that the ability to see things in different ways (Lesson 19) is an important aspect of the creative process, we can also see how it figures in the writing of stories, poems, skits, and essays. By promoting their students' ability to see things from different perspectives, teachers can enlarge their students' worlds and help them to become more tolerant people.

Each chapter of the book is devoted to a creative thinking skill in order to show how the skill can promote learning in the language arts. The creative thinking skills are already present in students, but in many cases they are undeveloped and even discouraged. For instance, the twelfth skill, enjoying and using fantasy (Lesson 12), is still frowned upon and stifled by many teachers because they believe it tends to encourage daydreaming and inattention, whereas the skill can be developed in the proper context and lead to learning that might not otherwise occur.

The materials in SPURS TO CREATIVE THINKING in Language Arts appeal to teachers because their students are challenged and entertained by them. Much of the motivation in the lessons comes from self-directed learning. In addition, the teacher is provided with a variety of ideas for following through with each lesson.

CONTENTS

For Bill and Linda McCleary
whose warm support
has encouraged me these many years

FOREWORD   by Dr. E. Paul Torrance

Almost all serious scholars of creative behavior agree that attitude and skills are important in creative achievement. Throughout his long career, R. E. Myers has been a master at stimulating the development of the attitudes and skills that facilitate creative achievements. This book is itself a creative achievement because, in ingenious ways, it spurs young people to use their intelligences. It affords students a great deal of practice in using creative and critical thinking skills as they work in this discipline.

In the fields of creativity testing, creative learning and teaching, and creative achievements in adult life, my associates and I have developed devices that aim to accomplish specific outcomes. We have regarded the following functions as most important in helping teachers and others do a better job: making teachers, psychologists, students, and parents aware of the most important creative abilities/skills that need to be developed or practiced; making them aware of the student's strengths for creative learning and problem solving; making them aware of gaps or deficits in the student's repertoire of creative abilities/skills; and providing a basis for generating evaluation procedures that assess not only the traditionally tested types of outcomes but also some of the more elusive objectives of education.

A list of abilities or skills follows and is elaborated on in my Making the Creative Leap Beyond and The Incubation Model of Teaching (Torrance 1999; Torrance and Safter 1990). The skills are all to be found in Myers's exercises in this book. I am sure that there are other creative abilities or skills, and some of those listed will in time be renamed.

finding the problem
producing alternatives (fluency)
being original
being flexible
elaborating
keeping open (delaying closure)
being aware of and using emotions
putting ideas into context
abstracting (highlighting the essence)

combining and synthesizing
visualizing richly and colorfully
fantasizing
using movement and sound
visualizing things internally
extending boundaries
using humor
respecting infinity
looking at things from a different perspective

I am also sure these abilities or skills will be called forth most effectively in response to the activities in this book and to the subject matter.

TO THE TEACHER

In the past 25 years a tremendous amount of writing has appeared in popular and professional publications concerning the nurturing of creativity. Whatever else has been said, or can be said, the attitudes that exist in any situation are the most important elements in creative production. In the classroom the attitude of the individual student, the attitude of the teacher, and the attitudes of the student's classmates concerning his or her ability to produce novel ideas are all-important.

If there is an attitude on the part of the student that his or her ideas are worthwhile, and if this attitude is reinforced by the student's teacher and classmates, positive things will happen, if only to the student's sense of self-worth. Conversely, no one is more vulnerable to harsh criticism than the person who reveals his or her original ideas, for those ideas tell everyone who he or she is.

Some clearheaded critics have noted the apparent paradox in the devising of methods, systems, programs, and the like for freeing up creative abilities. They point out, quite correctly, that these formulations are antithetical to the spirit of creativity. Our defense for books such as Spurs to Thinking is that through their use students and teachers alike often discover hidden talents in students who heretofore hadn't been known to have them.

Even a contrived activity in producing novel ideas is more conducive to the development of a talent, however slight, than is an exercise in repeating or retrieving someone else's information. In a perfect world, everyone could discover his or her talents by progressing through a series of experiences that would thereby inevitably help the individual to develop those talents. Our world often seems to be designed to discourage or even snuff out the talents of too many individuals. Spurs to Creative Thinking is an attempt to give the student an opportunity now and then to express ideas that might otherwise not be expressed.

Most educators nowadays agree that teachers are most effective in teaching thinking skills when the skills are employed naturally by students who are engaged in activities in the regular curriculum. That is why Spurs to Thinking consists of activities in social studies, language arts, science, and mathematics.

It is also apparent that more thinking skills are utilized when students are allowed to use their preferred sense modalities, thus assuring them of more success experiences in acquiring skills, abilities, and information. The current emphasis upon the importance of appealing to the many "intelligences" of young people is most welcome.

For more than three decades the author, in collaboration with E. Paul Torrance, has attempted to incorporate activities which involve young people in drawing, manipulating, acting, singing, dancing, constructing, touching, and interacting with all kinds of people. We have believed that the key to unlocking a child's potential is, and always has been, to allow him or her to succeed. By providing a wide range of opportunities for the young person to express herself or himself, a teacher can greatly increase the chance that she or he will succeed.

Although each of the activities that follows can be presented to your students in just the form in which it is given in this book, we encourage you to modify the activities in any way that makes them more appropriate, appealing, and/or effective in your classroom. It is obviously impossible for any author to write curriculum materials that suit all of the varieties of students found in today's classrooms. If you find something that is inappropriate or uninspiring, change it. Furthermore, if you somehow get an inspiration to take off on an idea in this book, please do so. Pursue your idea. These ideas should be considered spurs to your own thinking.

This book calls for all of Gardner's seven intelligences (Gardner, 1993; Armstrong, 1994) in a multimodal approach to stimulating learning. The emphasis, however, is upon the creative thinking skills described by E. Paul Torrance in Making The Creative Leap Beyond (1999). There has been an attempt to encourage each of those 18 skills in the activities that follow.

What we have attempted to do in this book is to give some very explicit procedures for encouraging students to think both creatively and critically. We have also provided a pedagogical framework that undergirds the activities. We hope to have explained the "why" as well as the "what" and "how" of using the units. These ideas for stimulating thinking can be presented by you at whatever occasions seem propitious. We ardently hope you will familiarize yourself with the lessons, noting the ones that seem likely to accomplish whatever objectives you have for your class during the year. A number of the lessons can be used on any occasion when you think they will foster learning. Others may be used most effectively when events and circumstances make their administration timely.

We have tried to select topics that will interest your students, but, not knowing them, we will probably miss the mark more than once. To ensure the success of those lessons you think may be most promising, we encourage you to modify and adapt them in your own way. It seems reasonable to us that, since you know your students, you can improve nearly everything in this book. We urge you to do so whenever you see the opportunity.

There are a great many activities in this book, and we don't expect you to use every one during a school year. Some call for advanced language skills, and others are more rudimentary. If they ignite any enthusiasm at all on the part of your students, a number of the lessons require several days or so to complete. You will find some units inappropriate for your students with respect to their interests, abilities, and backgrounds. We hope, however, that you will find quite a few that appeal to you because of their potential for motivating your students to think.

We believe in strongly encouraging young people to spell correctly, punctuate properly and effectively, and use good grammar when they write. In this book, there aren't many references to the formal aspects of writing, however. We don't mention first, second, and third drafts, but it is in rewriting that attention can be given to organization, grammar, punctuation, spelling, and syntax. Our reason for not emphasizing the mechanics of writing is that we hope to provoke original, spontaneous ideas and those are impeded when the individual is very much concerned with getting the words down correctly.

Spurs to Creative Thinking in Language Arts is not a "cook book" for enhancing the creative abilities of your students. With each unit we presume you will become a coauthor by leading into the unit with an anecdote, relevant object, pertinent question, or other warm-up device and by actually changing any activity so that it is more suitable for encouraging your students to think creatively and critically.

References

Armstrong, T. (1994) Multiple Intelligences in the Classroom. Alexandria, VA: Association for Supervision and Curriculum Development.

Gardner, H. (1993) Multiple Intelligences: The Theory in Practice. New York: Basic Books.

Torrance, E. P. and H. T. Safter. (1999) Making the Creative Leap Beyond. Buffalo, NY: Creative Education Foundation Press.

LESSON 1

"SENSITIVITY TO PROBLEMS"

Unless you are sensitive to what is taking place in your private world, as well as in the world at large, you won't be aware of how you can improve yourself or help others. Creative thinking begins with an **awareness of problems**.

Thinking skills emphasized

- **being sensitive, finding the problem**
- being original
- looking at it in another way
- combining and synthesizing
- making judgments
- hypothesizing

E. Paul Torrance (1999) maintains that creative thinking isn't likely to occur until there is an awareness of a problem, some definition of the problem, and a commitment to solve it. Further, he believes that when confronted with a perplexing problem an individual should be able to recognize the essence of the difficulty. To increase this skill, Torrance believes that it must be practiced.

Activity Thinking of Everyday Happenings and Writing a Report (45-50 minutes in class and time for research out of class)
Activity Sheet "Have You Noticed"

Preparing for the Activity

This kind of an activity is sometimes called a "sensitivity exercise." Its prime purpose is to encourage the individual to become more sensitive – more aware – of what is taking place around him. In the past 20 years or so, many activities have been devised to heighten the individual's powers of perception in a school setting. E. Paul Torrance has been particularly successful in having students carefully examine pieces of wood in order to sharpen their senses. They used <u>all</u> of their senses in gaining information – touching, smelling, tasting, seeing, listening. It is amazing how much information can be gained by a careful examination of small objects taken from nature. The tie-ins of this unit with science and art instruction are obvious. The unit can also be especially effective before and after field trips.

Administering the Activity

Two questions are posed at the beginning of the unit that are meant to get the student to thinking about everyday occurrences. These two questions, or ones like them, can be asked by you to warm up your students for the reflective thinking called for in the rest of this first section of the activity. A few of the questions that we present are likely to bring on some disagreements among your students. We hope they do. The activity is designed in a way that should make your students puzzle over what they experience every day, and at least a couple of their responses should be fairly tentative.

Your students are asked to check up on one or two of their responses regarding the opening of door knobs, taste of food, sunsets, etc. because it is easy to toss out an answer and let it go at that. Corroborating a statement or hypothesis requires some extra effort, but it is necessary in almost any venture we undertake. We have ruled you out as a source, hoping your students will go to parents, librarians, authorities, and most of all to the phenomena themselves in order to determine whether they are correct or not.

After gathering additional information, your students are likely to want to share what they have learned, especially in cases where they are right or where they learned something fascinating. This provides you an opportunity to go over some of the principles of report writing. Probably the best time to go over those points, however, is after first drafts (or even second drafts) have been written. It could stifle the enthusiasm of your youngsters if you were to stress form too much prior to their getting their findings down on paper.

Following Through

Some teachers (including the author) have had success designating able students as "editing helpers." By having these students assist other students, there are fewer interruptions and the class stays on task. The students in need of help don't have to wait for the teacher to finish a conference in order to get answers to their questions.

The initial requirement for a report is to gather facts. Accordingly, you should allow your students ample time for gathering, assembling, and organizing the facts needed to write an interesting report. To assist them in sharpening their focus on the report writing, you can give them a set of questions such as the following:

1. What topic appeals to me most?

2. How can I narrow that topic to a manageable size?

3. What is my purpose in writing this report?

4. Who is my audience (that is, other than the teacher)?

5. What main idea about my topic will accomplish my purpose and appeal to my audience?

6. How much do my readers already know about my topic?

7. What information will be interesting or useful to them?

8. What specific facts, sensory details, incidents, examples, and reasons can I use to develop my main idea?

HAVE YOU NOTICED?

1. How aware are you of the everyday happenings around you? Do you know when the street lights came on last night? If so, when was it? At what times and under what conditions does a voice carry farthest?

Here are eight common experiences that most of us have fairly often. Make an observation about each by completing the sentences below. There is not just one correct answer for any of the items. Answer in a way that is true for you.

   a. When I raise my hand in class, it is usually my _____ hand.

   b. One of the first sensations we have after a rainfall is _____

   c. Knobs on doors open _____

   d. Moths are attracted to light, but they don't flutter around an outdoor light as much

   _____

   e. The letters and numbers of <u>most</u> car license plates are _____

   f. We see sunsets because there are particles of various kinds in the air. This is especially apparent

   _____

   g. It is hard to get the true taste of food when _____

   h. The weather affects a piano by _____

2. You may be very sure of some of your statements above, but, even though you filled in the blanks, you may be less sure about others. Which one are you least sure about?

Check it out by asking an adult (but not your teacher). Is there another one that you have a little doubt about? If so, which one is it?

Find out if your statement is really correct, if you can. (One or two of your statements may be hard to check up on, such as the one about what happens after a rain.) Find out whether your statement is factual by testing, smelling, tasting, listening, or observing in some other way.

3. After you have done a good job of testing the accuracy of your statement, write what you did. Your report should be thorough enough to convince a reader that you have some evidence to support your statement. You can use the space on the next page to start your report.

Your statement

_____

(Title of Report) _____

(Finish the first draft of your report on as many other pages as you need to do a thorough job.)

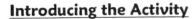

Alternate Activity
Listening Thoughtfully at Three Listening Posts and Writing Some Verse
(15 minutes outside; 45-50 minutes total for the activity)
Activity Sheet "Pick Your Spot"

Introducing the Activity

Select a time when your students are relatively settled and not jumpy in which to give them this activity. It works best when students are reflective and not skittish. Your students should profit from this opportunity to be quiet and take in the sounds at their "spots."

Administering the Activity

This activity will only work well if individual students are completely on their own. By trusting your students to leave the classroom and find themselves a place to record their aural observations, you will have done much to set the right tone for the activity. If the listening posts aren't too widely dispersed on the school grounds, it won't be hard for you to oversee your students, but you mustn't intrude. Check with your administration about rules for unsupervised out-of-classroom activities.

Upon returning to the classroom, your students can quietly set about putting their thoughts into verse. The results of this activity may well surprise you – and them.

Following Through

These are a few of the activities that you might have your students do after their experiences in the "Pick Your Spot" activity:

- Have your students share the most significant of their experiences.

- Have them rewrite (in good form) the verses and illustrate them.

- Have them use their verses for the lyrics to songs of their own composition.

- Have them put their impressions together under headings on the chalkboard. Headings might be "I was surprised by . . . ," "I'd never noticed before . . . ," "I got a kick out of . . . ," and the like.

PICK YOUR SPOT

1. Surely you have listened carefully many times during your life. You have listened intently when someone has given you important directions or instructions. You have listened attentively for the sound of approaching footsteps or an automobile when you waited for someone to meet you. You may also have listened nervously to the sounds of the night if you ever were awakened from your sleep. Now you are asked to listen carefully for a total of 15 minutes on the same day. You are to select three listening posts. At the first post you will listen for five minutes, and then you will move onto the second and third positions to listen for the same length of time. Do you think you will hear any sounds you have never heard before? Explain.

Do you expect to be bored by the three listening periods? Explain.

2. Find a good location for listening – any place where you can listen to sounds that interest you. Take a pencil and a notebook or pad along and write down everything that you think is unusual, surprising, fascinating, pleasing, upsetting, or in any way noteworthy. Next, move onto a spot where you will be near a group of people. Write down a brief description of anything you hear that is interesting to you. This time close your eyes during the entire five minutes. Leave your second position and find a third location where you will feel comfortable and inconspicuous. It may be a place where you are not observed by others, but you should not be "hiding." Record anything that seems noteworthy. This time close your eyes if you want.

Now, with the notes that you obtained during the three listening sessions, answer these questions:

    a. Which of the three positions was most satisfactory as a listening post? Why?
    b. Which method of listening was most productive – closed eyes or open eyes? Why do you think that way was superior to the other way?
    c. Did you learn more when people were nearby? Why?
    d. Was the first location that you selected actually a good listening post? In what ways was it a good or a poor place?
    e. Did you become a "sharper" listener by the time your three listening sessions were over? Explain.
    f. Would you have preferred to listen for a longer or a shorter period of time at any of the three locations? Why?
    g. Were you bored at any of the listening posts? If so, why?

3. Summarize the experience you had at one of the three listening posts in a limerick or a poem. Your notes can be the raw material with which you work to develop the poem or limerick.

Extensions

Activity Thinking of Ways to Improve the World and Writing an Essay (45-50 minutes) **Activity Sheet** "Nice and Quiet"

Introducing the Activity

This type of activity has been successful because young people are allowed to let their imaginations take wings while at the same time dealing with the real world. To introduce it, simply say that your students are to do some thinking about the world, and it should be fun because they are to imagine they have magical powers.

Administering the Activity

Although "Nice and Quiet" is meant to be administered to individual students, their responses should be shared with the group when they have answered all of the questions. This activity is of the kind that encourages students to be sensitive to problems. For example, the first question ("What would be nicer if it were quieter?") should bring forth some responses that are honest and probably worthwhile. (Be prepared to have someone respond, "Trudy" or "Reggie," however.) Because of the range of conditions that is called for in the questions, your students will be challenged to think deeply and widely.

Following Through

There are eight tips for writing an essay. You can add to the list, modify any of the tips, and/or substitute your own tips for those you don't like. If your students have been writing essays, this activity will serve as a way of giving them more practice. If they haven't done much essay writing, the eight tips should give them a good guide.

The essay writing could produce some thoughtful or humorous essays, and some of these can be reproduced in a student publication. Here are the eight points to keep in mind when students write an essay.

1. Know your audience. Adjust your language so that it is appealing and understandable to the audience.
2. Without being too obvious, establish your relationship with your audience. (What views do they share with you? What is common in your background with theirs?)
3. Give your audience a road map of where you are going in the essay, or at least make it clear that you have a message. Then try to make your message clear.
4. Get the audience's attention by means of a story, joke, reference to a recent event, and the like.
5. Repeat important ideas, but try to alter the language slightly in the repetition.
6. Use humor, but use it naturally.
7. What actions are you urging, if any? If your ideas are accepted by the audience, what should it do?
8. Reiterate your thesis in forceful and simple language at the end.

NICE AND QUIET

A. It seems to some of us that it would be mighty handy if we could change the world. There are many toys, gadgets, tools, conditions, and objects that might serve us better if we had the magic powers to change them. In this activity you will be given an opportunity to imagine that you can change things the way you would like to have them be. If you had the magic powers, what things would you change?

1. What would be nicer if it were quieter? Why? _____

_____

2. What would last longer if it were plastic? Why? _____

_____

3. What would be more comfortable if it were warmer? Why? _____

_____

4. What would be more humorous if it were invisible? Why? _____

_____

5. What would be prettier if it were blue? Why? _____

_____

6. What would be stronger if it were lighter? Why? _____

_____

7. What would be more valuable if it could float? Why? _____

_____

8. What would be more fun if it were faster? Why? _____

_____

9. What would be cleaner if it were electric? Why? _____

_____

10. What would be more efficient if it could go backwards? Why? _____

_____

B. Describe the changes which would take place in your life if you <u>were</u> able to effect one of the changes listed above. How would it affect other people?

C. Which of those changes would be best for you? _____

D. Which of those changes would be best for people generally? Put your ideas into the form of an essay.

LESSON 2

"TWO OR MORE"

We are told it is better to have more than one plan; it's a good idea to be able to fall back on "Plan B" when "Plan A" doesn't pan out. Similarly, it's to our advantage to be able to produce a number of ideas for a party; some of them may turn out to be excellent while others may be duds. So, often the person with many ideas is at an advantage over the person who is stuck on just one idea. In this lesson your students are asked to think of a great variety of alternatives. Another term for this skill is **fluency**.

> **Thinking skills emphasized**
>
> • **producing alternatives**
> • looking at it in another way
> • being original
> • analyzing
> • making judgments

The first principle of brainstorming (Parnes, 1992) is that there should be an atmosphere that will enable a group of people to generate a great many ideas. At first the quality of the ideas is not important – it's the number of ideas that matters. The theory behind this principle is that evaluation of the ideas can take place later on – better ideas typically come in the last half of a brainstorming session – and that there is a much better chance of getting a good idea or solution to a problem if there are a large number from which to choose. However, to be able to produce a lot of ideas, a participant has to be in the proper environment to do so. This means, for individuals in a brainstorming session or students in a classroom, that the participants must feel comfortable in expressing their ideas. As their teacher, you must show your students that it is psychologically safe for them to bring forth off-the-wall ideas.

Activity Producing Analogies and Writing Cinquains about Older People (45-50 minutes)
Activity Sheet "Analogies"

Introducing the Activity

A great deal of effort has been expended nowadays in education and elsewhere to give young people a better understanding of and appreciation for older people. An excellent way to introduce this activity is to project a film about the value of senior citizens. Two fine films, among the many that have been produced, are "Portrait of Grandpa Doc" (Phoenix/BFA) and "The Mailbox" (Brigham Young University). Both films are poignant stories about aging people, the first about a departed father/grandfather and grandfather/father and the second about an isolated grandmother/mother. You also might introduce this activity by briefly discussing an elderly person that your students are familiar with or by making a few comments about a senior you know well, perhaps a relative.

Administering the Activity

This is an activity that combines lessons about analogizing and writing cinquains. In the first part of the activity we offer some examples of how people are compared with other people, animals, and things. At the end of this part of the activity the student is asked to find an insect that might be compared to a younger brother.

The student is asked to produce four analogies at the second stage, and we have provided the forms for four different types of analogy. You will recognize them as metaphors and similes. Naming the types of analogy is not important for the purposes of this activity, and we don't care if your students follow the forms. If a student writes only similes, which is the easiest form to compose, we'll be just as happy. The metaphor, however, tends to bring the student closer to the notion put forth in the cinquain writing to come at the next level.

We offer the type of cinquain that follows a pattern of words, rather than syllables, because it is easier for students to master. The "pure" cinquain, invented by Adelaide Crapsey, has a 2-4-6-8-2 pattern of syllables for the five lines. Our example faithfully follows the 1-2-3-4-1 scheme of words, but it certainly isn't necessary for your students to adhere exactly to that pattern. An extra word here or a shorter line there is quite acceptable. The example given is about grandparents because there is always the danger that students will copy too closely a model that is held up as an example. We are sure you have been surprised several times by students giving you back, in only slightly altered form, what you offered simply as an illustration.

Following Through

Among the activities that could follow "Analogies" are those having to do with analogizing and others for producing cinquains. Analogies can be made among people, products, enterprises, or institutions that the young people know well. For example, they can compare professional athletes with computer whizzes, bus drivers with letter carriers, auto mechanics with doctors, teachers with preachers, and so forth.

Since cinquains are easy to compose, your students could write some about subjects that impinge upon their daily lives, such as the weather, holidays, their favorite foods, relatives, authors, singers, athletes, and the like. Challenge your more talented writers to try to use the word pattern simultaneously with the syllabic pattern (in other words, write 1, 2, 3, 4, and 1 words with 2, 4, 6, 8, and 2 syllables respectively for the five lines).

ANALOGIES

In order to make our ideas a little clearer, we often use comparisons. We compare people to other people ("My boss is another Hitler!"), animals ("Don't trust that weasel.") and things ("She's sweet as honey.") These comparisons are often in the form of similes (where the words "as" and "like" are used) or metaphors (where a likeness is implied rather than stated). If you were trying to describe an egotistical young man who dresses in a fancy way, you might compare him to a peacock: "The way he struts around like a peacock, he must be pretty stuck on himself."

We can get across an idea of what a person is like by making a comparison, or analogy. For instance, if you wanted to put over the idea of what younger brothers and sisters are like, you could compare them with puppies, kittens, poison ivy, glue, or leeches.

What insect is like a younger brother? _____

What insect is like a younger sister? _____

What insect is like an older brother? _____

What insect is like an older sister? _____

Compare younger brothers and sisters to whatever they remind you of in these four analogies.

First analogy A younger brother is like a _____

Second analogy A younger sister is a _____

because _____

Third analogy A younger brother _____

just as a _____

Fourth analogy Younger siblings are _____

If you have ever written cinquains, you know they aren't hard to write. You need only write 11 words! Here is an example of a cinquain that is based on the analogy of grandparents and gold mines.

One word title . . .   Mines

Two words, describing the title . . .   Family treasures

Three words expressing action . . .   For daily discovery

Four words expressing feelings . . .   Loving, sharing, caring, hoping

Another word for the title . . .   Grandparents

In the example above, the writer has drawn a comparison between grandparents and gold mines. In other words, this cinquain is kind of an analogy. As was done in the cinquain, some people like to reveal what the subject is in the last line, as a small surprise. Write one or two cinquains about people you know.

Alternate Activity Examining Metaphors and Producing Interpretations for Seven of Them (30-45 minutes) **Activity Sheet** "Some Moving Metaphors"

Introducing the Activity

A confusion between those two popular figures of speech, the simile and the metaphor, could provide a good chance to point out the distinctions between them and to present a lesson about metaphors. The point to be made about metaphors is that we use them all of the time without realizing it. Give a few examples of commonly used metaphors.

Administering the Activity

In one way, "Some Moving Metaphors" is brief, and it shouldn't take a full class period. On the other hand, it will be challenging to some, if not most, of your students because they have to produce as many interpretations of the seven sentences containing metaphors as they can. The lazy student may well settle for one or none, claiming the sentences are silly or confusing. Don't let her get away with it. Encourage her to <u>think</u>. Readers must make this kind of interpretation in the course of reading fiction or poetry. If they want to understand what they are reading, they have to make an effort to interpret metaphors. Intelligent reading requires both effort and imagination.

Following Through

Activities that could follow "Some Moving Metaphors" include:

• Have your students write a paragraph with at least one metaphor.
• Have your students look for metaphors in a passage they have just read in class, in a book they are reading for pleasure, in a textbook (literature and social studies are good bets), in the talk of people on television or at home, or in the talk of friends.
• Have them predict which will be the richest source of metaphors among those listed above.
• Have your students draw a picture of the misconception that a child has in trying to understand an expression such as "She flew off the handle." Give them a list to choose from for their illustrations of these misconceived metaphors. These are a few you can use:

    1. Sophie was stood up by her boyfriend.
    2. Mr. Gibson rocked Randy with the revelation.
    3. Jane's mother let her stew for awhile before telling her what really happened.
    4. The manager said this to the coach about their star pitcher: "Sid's got it! He's really smoking today!"
    5. Jon stole his thunder.
    6. "Don't bother me," said the writer. "I don't want to stop now that my motor's running."
    7. The man flew into a rage when he got the bill.
    8. The situation was complicated, and Jerry just muddied the waters when he tried to explain it.

SOME MOVING METAPHORS

Although you may not realize the extent to which you use them, metaphors comprise an important part of your working language. Expressions such as "He ran roughshod over his competition," "The inspector sniffed out the crucial clue," and "She wove a tangled web of lies" are found in many people's conversation or writing.

Here are seven sentences with metaphors. What events, natural phenomena, objects, institutions, or abstractions might be described by these sentences? List as many as you can for each sentence, but don't include animals or people.

1. They just flew by.

_____

2. Relentlessly, a little at a time, it ate away at what was left.

_____

3. Instead of flowing, it crawled along.

_____

4. It just chews you up!

_____

5. That enabled her to throw off the shackles of guilt.

_____

6. Never still, always creeping forward, it threatened everything around.

_____

7. Its shadowy arches rose higher and higher.

_____

Extensions

Activity Game of Analogies (15-20 minutes)

In small groups or with the entire class, have your students respond orally to a dozen analogies. The teacher, or leader, has a copy of the analogies given below and reads the first to the group, calling on the student whose hand is raised first. If she has an answer the group considers correct, the student reads the next analogy on the list, and so on. An individual can respond to all 12 analogies, but she should be limited to only one turn of reading the next analogy.

The leader should allow for discussion if there is any question as to the correct answer. There may be more than one correct answer, and often there is room for doubt, as in an analogies test. The author of the test can overlook a valid relationship.

Although your students are probably familiar with the structure of the typical analogy on a test, you can give this example:

"An <u>author</u> is related to a <u>book</u> in the same way that a <u>composer</u> is related to . . . <u>a piece of music</u> (a musical composition)." Show your students on the chalkboard that the analogy will look like this:

author: book   composer: _____

Most of the analogies are on the easy side to ensure maximum participation on the part of your students. If you want to challenge them more, please substitute harder ones. These are the answers – at least I suppose they are correct.

1. noodles, rice (Asian food)   2. hands

3. cake   4. villain

5. magnet   6. tragedy

7. Foal   8. thermometer

9. drought   10. village, small town

11. land   12. Jack

COMPARING WITH ANALOGIES

1. fork : spaghetti

        (utensils for eating food)

        chopsticks : _____

2. socks : feet

        (coverings for extremities)

        gloves : _____

3. attic : house

        (top and whole)

        frosting : _____

4. wet : dry

        (opposites)

        hero : _____

5. moth : flame

        (attraction)

        iron : _____

6. hard : soft

        (opposites)

        comedy : _____

COMPARING WITH ANALOGIES

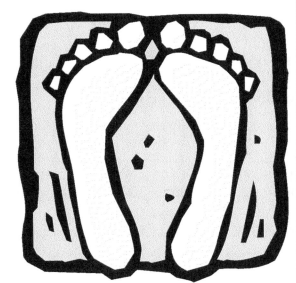

7. adult : baby   (birthing)

       horse : _____

8. inches : ruler   (units of measure and instruments for measuring)

       degrees : _____

9. slow : fast   (opposites)

       flood : _____

10. belly laugh : chuckle   (contrast in size)

       metropolis : _____

11. hurricane : water   (where storm originated)

       tornado : _____

12. Gretel : Hansel   (girl-boy combinations)

       Jill : _____

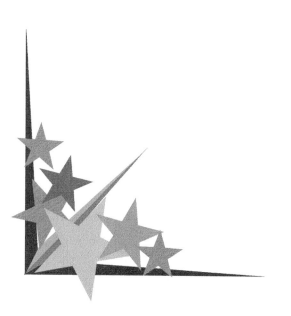

Activity Producing Alternative Ways of Accomplishing a Variety of Tasks
(45-50 minutes)
Activity Sheet "De-Furring the Feline"

Preparing for the Activity

This activity calls for your students to think of ways to do a wide variety of tasks, most of them from their everyday lives. Look the tasks over before handing out the activity. If any of them don't seem appropriate, don't hesitate to substitute more suitable ones.

Administering the Activity

"De-Furring the Feline" is structured so that, after a brief introduction, the student is put on her own. The last part, however, has her getting together with another student in comparing their ideas about accomplishing the prescribed tasks. You might have a brief general discussion afterward. Allow about 10-15 minutes for the discussion.

Following Through

Depending upon how your students react to "De-Furring the Feline," you might follow its completion with another activity like it at another time. They will understand that there are two or more ways to do almost anything.

Notes

DE-FURRING THE FELINE

The old saying "There is more than one way to skin a cat" reminds us that there is often more than one way to accomplish a task. There are many ways to start a fire, skip a rock, tie a necktie, fold a napkin, and comb your hair. Do you do things the same way every time?

What are the advantages and disadvantages of always doing something the same way?

Advantages

_____

_____

_____

_____

Disadvantages

_____

_____

_____

_____

What are two ways of calling a dog?

1. _____

2. _____

Can you think of another way? What is it?

_____

Describe two ways of tearing a piece of paper exactly in half. Illustrate the two methods.

Describe two ways of eating a bunch of grapes. Demonstrate to the class the two ways.

_____

_____

_____ or you can _____

_____

_____

What are two ways of preserving the color of an autumn leaf? If you can, illustrate the two methods.

1. _____

2. _____

Describe two ways of catching a frog. Make a diagram of the two ways.

What are two ways of capturing a melody that occurs to you?

1. _____

2. _____

Can you think of another way? What is it?

Describe two ways of measuring half-way between two points without a ruler or tape measure. Illustrate the two methods.

What are two ways of putting a pillow case on a pillow? Diagram each way.

What are two ways of remembering the name of someone you have just met?

1. _____

2. _____

Is there another way? What is it?

_____

Was it harder to describe how to do the tasks in words, or was it more difficult to illustrate your methods? Explain.

_____

_____

_____

_____

Compare your ways of accomplishing the tasks above with someone else's. Find out if that person has an interesting way of tackling the job that you hadn't thought of. What did you learn?

Activity Making Up Appositives and Writing a Character Sketch (45-50 minutes) **Activity Sheet** "In Apposition"

Introducing the Activity

Although the appositive is probably not high on your list of grammatical lessons to be taught, the construction is quite common and should be understood by your students. Accordingly, you can feel justified in administering this lesson even though its real purpose is to get your students to write a character sketch.

You might introduce the activity by saying: **Do you remember what an appositive is? It's kind of a fussy word that grammarians use, but you undoubtedly know what one is. (A word or group of words that extends the meaning of a word or phrase next to it.)**

It would be surprising if your students became excited about learning about appositives, but you can bring them along by asking who "Benny the Dip," "Pete the Scoring Machine," and "Dino the Dinosaur" might be. (You probably can come up with better examples.)

Administering the Activity

The first part of the activity was meant to be administered to individual students, but it can also be given to the class as a whole. You can take responses from class members and have the class decide which are the most effective appositives for persons they know (mother, teacher, friend, rival, and salesperson) and then for people they don't know personally (actor, actress, singer, athlete, and politician).

Once students understand appositives, ask your students to use two appositives in a character sketch. They are given some guidance about writing a character sketch, but you can go into it more deeply if you wish.

If you would like to give your students additional instruction in writing a character sketch, "Grandpa, My Favorite Relative" is perhaps a more complete breakdown of the genre than is necessary, and you may wish to streamline it. It is offered mainly to show how the elements can be organized in the sketch.

Notes

IN APPOSITION

The definition of an <u>appositive</u> is that it is a word or group of words that extends the meaning of a word or phrase next to it. Grammarians consider appositives as clauses in which the pronoun and verb are omitted. For example, in "Mr. Jordan, (who is) Henry's uncle, was a bus driver," we ordinarily would leave out "who is." These are other examples of appositives.

Bubby, our dog

Tom, his constant companion

Henry, the league's scoring leader

Benny, the head waiter at the Ritz

Paul Givens, the Emmy-award-winning actor

Salem, the capital of Oregon

Mervin, the village idiot

Krider's Drug Store, the meeting place for the gang

The key to knowing that a group of words is an appositive is that it is found next to the word or phrase it refers to. Usually the appositive is preceded or followed by a comma, but sometimes a name and an appositive are run together, as in Freddy the Freeloader, Alexander the Great, and Richard the Lion-Hearted.

Appositives are very useful in telling about people in a few words. You've probably used them in your writing a number of times without giving them much thought. Think of several appositives for people you know. Write appositives for (1) your mother, (2) a teacher, (3) a friend, (4) a rival, and (5) someone who sells you things.

1. _____

2. _____

3. _____

4. _____

5. _____

Now write appositives for some people you don't know personally: (1) an actor, (2) an actress, (3) a singer, (4) an athlete, and (5) a politician.

6. _____

7. _____

8. _____

9. _____

10. _____

Are all of your 10 appositives effective in telling about someone in just a few words? Which one is the most effective? Why do you think it is the most effective of the 10 appositives?

Incorporate one or two appositives in a sketch of someone you know well. This kind of writing is sometimes called a character sketch.

There are just a few things to keep in mind as you write your sketch. Most importantly, try to capture the essential nature of your subject. What is distinctive about the indi- vidual? Physical appearance is important in sketching a person, but you should work the description of what he or she looks like into the first paragraph or so and not devote a paragraph entirely to that aspect.

Some background about the person's life is desirable, but don't write more than a paragraph about his or her history. There should be some details about what the person does – whether he or she is a student or what kind of job the person has.

Quite a bit of your sketch should deal with the individual's personality. This can be done in several ways. Among them could be remarks about how the person relates to friends, family members, and associates. Another way to reveal a good deal about a person is to quote him or her, which also shows how he or she talks; this gives a flavor to the sketch that can't be obtained otherwise.

ELEMENTS OF A CHARACTER SKETCH

Purpose: The primary purpose of a character sketch is to inform, but it can also be to impress or entertain the reader or to praise the subject.

Subject: You should select someone you know quite well as the subject, and that person should also be interesting to your readers.

Audience: You should bear in mind the ages, backgrounds, and interests of your readers.

Subject's Characteristics: The facts, traits, idiosyncrasies, and accomplishments of the subject provide the fabric of the character sketch. Anecdotes and quotes are also helpful in portraying the subject. Your purpose in writing the sketch will determine which of those details are included.

Emphasis: You can stress the subject's personality, appearance, character, or accomplishments.

Organization: A character sketch has an introduction, middle section, and close. The introduction contains one or two of the most important traits of the subject. The middle section contains more details and also provides a revealing glimpse of the subject. The close summarizes the subject's personality or character.

Revision: Examine your first draft with a critical eye. Look especially to see if your sketch gives the reader a clear picture of your subject. It helps a great deal to have another person read your second draft in an objective way. Ask yourself if you are satisfied with the final draft.

MY FAVORITE RELATIVE

Opening statement/facts

_____

_____

_____

Appearance/facts

_____

_____

_____

Personality trait

_____

_____

_____

Glimpse of subject

_____

_____

_____

Personality trait/examples

_____

_____

_____

Personality trait/examples

_____

_____

_____

Personality trait/examples

_____

_____

_____

_____

Facts

_____

_____

_____

_____

Quote

_____

_____

_____

_____

Summary statement/

_____

_____

_____

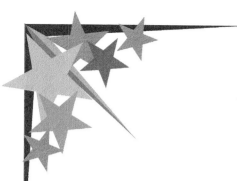

Example

Grandpa, My Favorite Relative

Opening statement/facts

Appearance/facts

Personality trait

My favorite relative was a fighter pilot in World War II, and he's only 5'4" tall. But those 64 inches weigh a solid 185 pounds. Even though Grandpa is 79, you'd guess he couldn't be more than 65. Maybe he was blond when he was young, but now his hair is silvery white. There's usually a twinkle in his eye and a half-smile on his face. He looks like a good-natured gnome. Grandpa cracks jokes all the time, but sometimes they aren't very funny. That's all right – he tries.

Glimpse of subject

Personality trait/
example
Personality trait/example

When I go over to visit my grandparents, Grandpa is usually busy at his workbench in the garage. He can fix almost anything. Once, when I was young, he fixed my train set when Dad couldn't. The other day he was able to fix the muffler on my car. He just works away at whatever he's doing, but when I ask him a question he likes to explain how things work.

Personality trait/example

Facts

Quote

Grandpa doesn't talk much about his experiences in World War II or about being a high school principal, and he doesn't try to give me advice. He's a great fisherman because he's patient. Maybe that's why he has been married to Grandma for 49 years. During that time she went from being a flaming liberal to a diehard conservative. When someone asked Grandpa why he put up with Grandma's political shenanigans and occasionally bizarre behavior, he said: "Maybe it's because I love her."

Summary Statement/
example

Even though he doesn't tell me what to do, I like to talk with Grandpa when I have a problem. He doesn't tell me I goofed or anything. Mostly he just listens. I guess that's why he's my favorite relative and one of my very favorite people.

Reference

Parnes, S.J. (1992). Source Book for Creative Problem-Solving: A Fifteen Year Digest of Tested Intellectual Process. Buffalo, N.Y.: Creative Education Foundation Press

LESSON 3

"QUICK THINKING"

Occasionally we find ourselves in a situation that calls for solving a problem that has never confronted us before. The situation may be serious or not, but it challenges us to see how its elements relate to one another in ways that are essentially new to our experience. This activity will test your students' ingenuity.

> Thinking skills emphasized
>
> - **being flexible**
> - producing alternatives
> - being original
> - visualizing richly and colorfully
> - analyzing
> - making judgments

The main skill to be called for in this lesson is **flexible thinking**. It can be regarded as the opposite of rigid thinking. In (1999), E. Paul Torrance remarks that J.P. Guilford defined flexible thinking operationally. Guilford recognized different kinds of flexibility. This kind of flexibility involves spontaneously changing a mental set for doing something. This is what is called "breaking the set." Guilford also found that there is an adaptive aspect to flexibility. For example, in the Torrance Tests of Creative Thinking the subjects are asked to think of improving a stuffed toy (e.g., making it into a cookie container or candy dispenser, to change its function). If they make it something other than a stuffed toy, they are using adaptive flexibility.

It is plain that people are both rigid and flexible when it comes to their daily routines and their approaches to social problems, but it is not quite so obvious that they can be flexible and inflexible in the way they think of ordinary objects. For example, a paper clip is to many people something for attaching papers together and not much else; but to other people it is something with which to make decorations, to poke holes, to tie tire chains together, to trace curves, ad infinitum. When the occasion demands, we can redefine commonplace objects and solve the little problems that confront us – if we are flexible in our thinking and not rigid in the way we perceive the objects around us. An inability to see more than one use for an object is called functional fixity, whereas the ability to see different kinds of uses for an object is termed semantic spontaneous flexibility.

An ability that is closely related to semantic spontaneous flexibility is that of figural spontaneous flexibility. This is the ability to see rapid alternatives in perceived visual figures. For instance, do you see first one and then another square as you look at this outline cube?

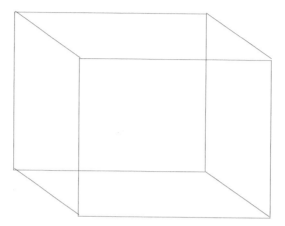

You are probably familiar with other examples of figural flexibility such as the old-crone-and-the-young-girl drawing. The fascinating thing about these ambiguous figures is that sometimes when you alternate from one perception it is hard to return to your original perception.

There are many jobs which require the individual to adapt spontaneously to varying situations. One of these jobs is teaching. Each day situations arise that necessitate thinking on the part of the teacher which is flexible and adaptable. Frequently, to be rigid is to invite misunderstanding, hurt feelings, and/or failure. Similarly, the student who is unable to change his approach to a problem will undoubtedly have trouble. Flexibility is an important dimension of teaching as well as of thinking.

Activity Solving Practical Problems That Require Ingenious Solutions (45-90 minutes)
Activity Sheet "Predicaments"

Introducing the Activity

You might introduce the activity by saying something like the following: **There are times when each of us finds herself or himself in a situation that requires some quick thinking. What follows are four situations that call for some ingenious thinking.**

Distribute the activity sheet. Give your students a chance to read about the seven predicaments, and then ask if they have any questions. To warm them up for thinking in a flexible way, you might describe how you solved a practical problem at home, or perhaps relate the experience of the man who fell off a ladder when cleaning a gutter on the garage, thereby smashing his shoulder and breaking his arm. His wife then forbade him to get on a ladder again, but the gutter was clogged up badly the following autumn. Since the gutter was

40

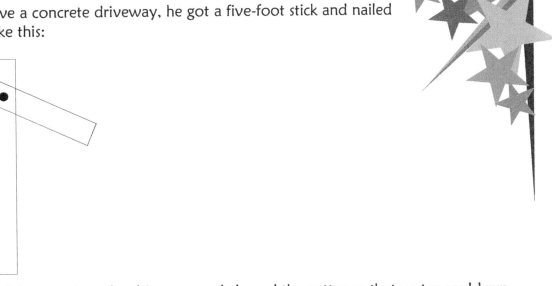

about nine feet above a concrete driveway, he got a five-foot stick and nailed another stick to it like this:

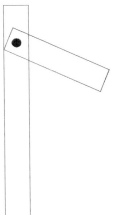

With this simple tool, he stood on the driveway and cleared the gutter so that water could run down the drain pipe once more, and he didn't have to use the treacherous ladder.

Administering the Activity

Your students can tackle the four problems singly or in groups of two or four. There may be some students – or some group – that have very few ideas, and so you should encourage them to brainstorm solutions if that technique seems promising. If there are four in a group, have the group designate a spokesperson.

After the majority of the class has finished or come close to finishing the activity, bring the class together and ask for their solutions to the problems. After one or two have been offered, you might set up some criteria for evaluating the solutions with your students. If this part of the activity requires more time than 45 minutes, the evaluation can be deferred to another period. These are criteria that might be applied to the four problems:

- Have you heard of a similar predicament that was solved in this way?

- Is the solution practical in terms of the conditions specified?

- Will you have enough time to solve the problem in this way?

- Will you have enough resources available to use this solution?

Following Through

A natural way of following up this lesson is for your students to suggest three or four predicaments to be solved by the class. Encourage them to describe situations in which someone they know or they themselves have been involved and either solved or failed to solve the problem.

PREDICAMENTS

It's hard to avoid finding yourself occasionally in a spot where you are hard-pressed to know what to do next. With all the good intentions in the world, you can find yourself choosing between hurting someone's feelings and committing yourself to an hour or a day or longer of doing what you hate to do. For instance, a good friend says she is in terrific need of someone to supervise the little kids at a party, and you greatly dislike being with youngsters with runny noses who always have to go to the bathroom. In a predicament like that, you'll probably just have to suffer unless you can quickly think of an excuse.

Here are seven other situations that call for some quick thinking. How would you handle each of them?

1. There are only five seats in your family's car, and your father and mother always sit in the front. In getting ready to go to a game, they have offered to give a ride to twins, who you can't stand – neither of them! That means you will either have to sit with the twins or not go to the game. Is there a solution? What will you do?

2. You come home and find no one else is there. A note from your mother says she won't be home until after 9:00 and for you to fix your own dinner. You look in the refrigerator and find only liver, which you hate, and some vegetables you wish your mother hadn't bought. Nothing there appeals to you. Since you are completely broke, you can't go out to get some food. What will you do?

3. After hoping you would be invited to join a club, you happily attend your first meeting. Midway through the meeting the president asks for volunteers to sell tickets to the fundraiser coming up. Four hands go up, but the president says that five people are needed for the job – and looks right at you. You are really quite shy with people you don't know, and you hate to ask anyone to spend money. Will you raise your hand? What can you do?

4. For quite awhile everyone you know has been really looking forward to a concert. A week before the concert a friend asks you if you'd like to attend it with the friend and a couple of others. Before you can reply, a teacher interrupts and asks both of you to help her move a large table into her room. Then the bell rings, and everyone heads for a desk. At the end of the period another friend, who you like a little better than the one who invited you to go with a group to the concert, invites you to go to the concert with a different group of friends. You feel obligated somehow to the first friend, who asked you before class, but you would rather go with the second friend and that group. What should you do?

5. Generally speaking, you like everyone in your class. However, there have been a couple of feuds going on all year between a few individuals. At recess one day, when you have permission to stay in the room and finish a project, you hear two of your classmates talking outside the door. The transom had been opened at the top of the door, and you can hear them quite distinctly. They are planning to put itching powder in the gym clothes of a classmate they dislike. You wonder whether you should warn that classmate or somehow try to talk the two students out of their plan. The problem is, you'd be embarrassed to let them know that you were eavesdropping. What should you do?

6. You saw a lovely sweater in the window of your favorite store and then begged your mother all week for money to buy it. Finally she relented, and you hurried down to the store and bought the sweater on Saturday. You came to school on Monday and were quite disturbed to see a friend wearing the identical sweater. Since she is a good friend, and since wearing your new sweater to school on another day would be embarrassing to her, you are in a quandary. What should you do?

7. You are introduced by your father's boss to an attractive individual about your age as "Chris," when your name is "Kim." There are many people in the group gathered around your father's boss because he is being honored at a dinner. You'd like the person to know your real name, but you are hesitant to correct your father's boss, who should know your name because he's known you for years. What should you do?

Extension

Activity Sheet "Catching a Water Beetle" (45-50 minutes)

Introducing the Activity

If the "Predicaments" activity generates sufficient thinking and learning, you can follow up with an activity about catching a water beetle. This activity requires similar problem-solving skills to that of "Predicaments." Your students will have to be flexible in their thinking again. You might introduce it by saying: **If you felt somewhat fascinated by the problems we've been solving in "Predicaments," here is another one like those. Some of you may have tried to catch a tadpole or a minnow, and that might help you in coming up with an idea for "Fred" in this story. See if you can produce a really good idea.**

Administering the Activity

The same criteria that were developed for the "Predicaments" solutions can be applied to the solutions offered in "Catching a Water Beetle." You can group your students in light of their performances in "Predicaments." That is, if dyads or groups of four worked well, the students could remain in the same groups. If not, it might be better to have the students work individually.

Following Through

Since this activity deals with a more rural aspect than do most of the others in this book, you might continue the theme of catching small creatures in ponds, creeks, fields, and trees by having a discussion about the best ways to entrap the animals. By no means is it suggested here that your students should kill small creatures, however. Recommend that, with the exception of sincere collectors, your students should release the little animals after they are examined. If Gardner (1993) is correct, many young people have an intelligence regarding nature that should be developed.

Notes

CATCHING A WATER BEETLE

Fred was stumped. He didn't know what to do. His teacher had asked him to catch a water beetle. She knew there was a pond near Fred's home. So she asked him to find a water beetle in the pond. Fred was unhappy because each time he tried to scoop up a water beetle, it got away.

Water beetles can breathe under water because they catch air underneath their bodies. They use the air for breathing when they are under the water. They have flat legs for swimming.

Water beetles are also quick. Quicker than Fred. He kept trying to catch a water beetle in a jar. He couldn't catch one. Then he tried a larger jar. Still no luck. Finally, Fred used a two-gallon bucket. That didn't work either.

Fred was about to give up when he had an idea. "That might work," Fred said out loud.

What was Fred's idea?

_____

_____

_____

_____

_____

_____

_____

_____

_____

Role Playing

You might also have your students engage in an exercise that calls for spontaneous flexibility. First, give them the following story orally:

Glynnis thought it would be a great idea to have an end-of-the-year picnic in the park two blocks from school. She enthusiastically invited her friends, telling them that she'd provide all the food and drinks. She decided to get box lunches from the deli and several quarts of soft drinks from the market nearby. On Saturday noon, the day after school closed, she arrived at the park and set out blankets on the grass just before three of her friends arrived. After exchanging greetings, Keesha, one of her friends, asked Glynnis whether everyone was there. Glynnis said that Mabel was coming too, and just after that Mabel came on the scene – but she was with Janice.

Glynnis turned white. She had forgotten that she had also invited Janice, and there were just five box lunches! What can Glynnis do?

You can very briefly stop the action at the point of Glynnis's realization of her gaffe and have the student portraying "Glynnis" actually do the problem solving, or you can let the class offer suggestions.

It might be a good idea if there are two groups of students taking the roles. The second group of role players can be removed from the class so that they don't hear any of the solutions to the problems.

Allow 35 to 50 minutes for role playing and problem solving.

References

Gardner, H. (1993). Multiple Intelligences: The Theory in Practice. New York: Basic Books.

Torrance, E. P. and H. T. Safter (1999). Making the Creative Leap Beyond. Buffalo, N.Y.: Creative Education Foundation Press.

Notes

LESSON 4

"DOING IT YOUR WAY"

When free of pressure, it is natural for young people to interact with their environments in novel and productive ways. In this lesson they are gently led to places where it is not too scary or uncomfortable to express their individuality. They shouldn't feel self-conscious as they express their ideas in these activities.

> **Thinking skills emphasized**
>
> - **being original**
> - combining and synthesizing
> - producing alternatives
> - analyzing
> - making judgments

Originality is the hallmark of creativity. Something that's not original is, by its nature, not very creative. Teaching someone to be creative, however, is another matter entirely. It's almost a contradiction in terms. In this lesson we want to give your students the opportunity to be creative. There is no guarantee that all of them will produce something original, but we hope that many of your students will be stimulated to do so by responding to the ideas in the activities.

Activity Writing Cinquains (35-45 minutes)
Materials pencils, crayons, felt pens, colored chalk
Activity Sheet "Thoughts"

Introducing the Activity

The original cinquain was written in a syllable pattern of 2-4-6-8-2, but it is easier for most teachers to use the simpler 1-2-3-4-1 word pattern for the five lines. Even though the purist pronounces cinquain as a French word, it is quite all right to say "Sin-kwayne." You can introduce the activity by letting your students know that they'll be writing some very short verses. (Avoid the term "poem.") They don't take long, and they are fun to do.

Administering the Activity and Following Through

When your students have written their cinquains, you might engage them in one or more of the following activities:

- Have the class write a cinquain as a group effort.
- Have your students decorate their cinquains with drawings and designs.
- Have a committee put together the cinquains that are produced in a booklet.
- Display the cinquains.
- After the cinquains have been circulated or seen, have your students select one or two for a student publication.
- Challenge your students to find out who originated the cinquain and when that person did so. It is not an ancient French form. Adelaide Crapsey created it early in the twentieth century in imitation of the dwarf forms of poetry loved by the Japanese.

If the activity is successful, you can have your students write more. They can choose from topics such as sports, holidays, TV programs, computers, foods, and countless others – or choose a topic of their own.

The reasons that young people apparently enjoy writing cinquains is that they are easy to write, and there aren't many words to write. They can follow the prescription for each line and feel rather secure that the whole affair is coming off all right.

Notes

THOUGHTS

1. Boys and girls like all kinds of things – spiders, clowns, fishing, a game of tag, rockets, baking cakes and cookies, gum, puzzles, puppies, ice cream, reading, bikes, hikes, television, talking, and much more. But everyone doesn't like the same things. Pick three things you like most and tell why you enjoy them so much.

a. I like _____ because _____

b. I like _____ because _____

c. I like _____ because _____

2. What do you like to do in the morning?

_____

_____

_____

What do you like to do on Saturdays?

_____

_____

_____

What do you like to do on Sundays?

_____

_____

_____

What do you like to do after school?

_____

_____

_____

What do you like to think about?

_____

_____

_____

What makes you happiest of all?

_____

_____

_____

3. Pick one of the things you enjoy most and arrange your thoughts like this.

Noon	**(one word, the subject)**
Eating time	**(two words about the subject)**
Munching, crunching, eating	**(three words of action)**
I love noon time	**(four words of feeling)**
Lunch	**(another word for the subject)**

This <u>cinquain</u> (a little poem of five lines) was written by astudent. You can see that each line has one more word than the one before, except for the last line. Cinquains can be written about almost any subject. You can use the space below to write your cinquain.

_____

_____

_____

_____

Extensions

Activity Playing a Rhyming Game and then Writing Limericks (30-50 minutes)
Activity Sheet "Five Lines"

Introducing the Activity

By reading one of Edward Lear's classic limericks, your students will be in the mood for "Five Lines." The rhythm of a limerick is vital to its effectiveness, and so your reading a limerick aloud will refresh your students' memories of its form and of its humor.

Administering the Activity

It might be a good idea to do the rhyming exercise at the beginning of "Five Lines" as a class activity. Give your students a chance to respond to the 10 prompts on their own, and then ask for volunteers to offer their rhymes. Probably 10 minutes is enough time for the class to come up with most of their answers. Some students will be stumped and unable to think of more than two or three rhymes. By allowing the quick ones to respond to the tough prompts, the slow ones won't be made uncomfortable, but they'll get the idea.

These are possible answers to the rhyming game:

- very warm child = hot tot
- young Helvetian lady = Swiss miss
- celebrity's automobiles = star's cars
- bovine's disputes = cow's rows
- avian art lover = culture vulture
- fat hunting dog = round hound
- cautious songbird = wary canary
- moist airplane = wet jet
- evil clergyman = sinister minister
- stuck-up Robert = snobby Bobby

Following Through

Limericks can be written about any number of subjects, and so a follow-up activity of "Five Lines" could be an assignment to produce one or more limericks about a chosen topic that is being studied. If your students are studying a social problem, an author, a species of animal or plant, space exploration, or inflation, they can contrive five lines that will provoke some merriment and also say something about the topic.

Activity Inventing Onomatopoetic Words (20-30 minutes)
Activity Sheet "Bang, Clang, Twang"

FIVE LINES

A. The <u>limerick</u> is a beloved, and often maligned, form of light verse. It is not poetry, nor does a writer of limericks pretend to be a poet when he or she writes five lines of mirth. The two principal ingredients of the limerick are <u>rhyme</u> and <u>humor</u>. A limerick that doesn't make some claim to being humorous, however slight, is not really a limerick.

Possibly the reason there are so many limericks being written is that people enjoy writing them. Maybe the fun in writing a limerick is greater than the fun in reading or hearing one. The enjoyment arises partially because limericks are easy to write.

Let's prove the truth of that last statement. To get you in the mood to write a limerick, play this simple game. Translate the words on the left into two words that rhyme. To illustrate, if we give you the phrase "sad friend," you could respond "glum chum."

1. very warm child _____ _____

2. fat hunting dog _____ _____

3. young Helvetian lady _____ _____

4. cautious songbird _____ _____

5. celebrity's automobiles _____ _____

6. moist airplane _____ _____

7. bovine's disputes _____ _____

8. evil clergyman _____ _____

9. avian art lover _____ _____

10. stuck-up Robert _____ _____

B. Let's say that somehow you come up with "snobby Bobby" for number 10. You might think of other rhyming words to go with that pair, such as hobby, knobby, lobby, and so forth. Your limerick might then turn out to be something like this:

There was a young lad named Bobby
Who had a mischievous hobby;
He teased little girls
By pulling their curls
Until they became mad and sobby.

Often the last line is a surprise. (The limerick above doesn't have that virtue.)

As you can see, a limerick's first, second, and fifth lines end in rhymes, as do the third and fourth lines (in a different rhyme). Write one or two, perhaps using some of the rhyming words you have come up with in the game you have just played. If those rhymes don't work, use any that come into your head. You know . . . head, bed, sled, red, shed, and so on and on.

BANG, CLANG, TWANG

We have a great variety of words that imitate the sounds we commonly hear in our homes, on the streets, and in the country. Words such as "bang," "twang," "plop," "gurgle," "poof," "chirp," "clank," "buzz," "slurp," "whack," and "thud" are representative of this type of word, which is called <u>onomatopoeia</u>. Many of the sounds we hear most often already have had words invented for them and are used in the world's languages. It is quite likely that words such as "poof," "smack," "ping," and "pop" will remain in English as long as the language is spoken.

There must be quite a few sounds we frequently hear, however, that do not as yet have words associated with them. Can you come up with words that imitate these sounds?

1. the rubbing of a tree or bush against the side of a building _____

2. the blowing out of air from the mouth when someone is greatly relieved _____

3. the rapid beating of a mosquito's wings near your ear _____

4. the tearing open of an envelope _____

5. the end of a yawn by a large dog _____

6. the skidding of a bicycle just before it slides out from under the rider _____

You probably can think of other sounds for which we have no accepted words to represent them. Think of a sound in each of these three categories that doesn't have an onomatopoetic word associated with it, and then give it an appropriate word that imitates the sound. Check with a dictionary to make sure your words are original.

a sound from a DVD player _____

a sound from a kitchen utensil _____

a sound from a traffic jam _____

LESSON 5

"AT THE HEART"

We recognize the value of those people who can get "right to the heart" of a problem. This lesson is concerned with giving your students some practice in using that important skill.

> **Thinking skills emphasized**
>
> - **highlighting the essence**
> - being original
> - letting humor flow
> - analyzing
> - making judgments

Torrance (1999, p. 105) notes that a cartoonist on the editorial page of a newspaper practices the skill of **highlighting the essence** every working day. He takes a story, with all its complexities, or a set of news stories, and tries to capture the essence of all this information in a cartoon. In a real way, the cartoonist couldn't make a living without the skill.

Activity Thinking of Nicknames for Holidays and Days of the Week
(30-40 minutes)
Activity Sheet "Chicken Little Day"

Introducing the Activity

Since there seems to be a tendency to create more national holidays, why shouldn't there be a "Chicken Little Day?" Although this isn't offered seriously – and the activity should be engaged in lightheartedly – making up nicknames for holidays is a legitimate pastime. You can say to your students: **Let's see how good you are at making up names. Can you think of a nickname for a beauty contest?** (Powder Puff Derby, Smile-a-thon, Talent Troop, and the like could be offered.) **Here is a chance to do some nicknaming.**

Administering the Activity

The nicknaming of people is a kind of **highlighting the essence** activity. Nicknames come closer to getting at the essential nature of a person than their legal names, of course, since very few Taylors sew and very few Carpenters swing a hammer. One slow-moving young man

I knew was called "Speedy" wherever he went, although the new group in which he found himself was unaware that he'd been called that by others.

If you administer "Chicken Little Day" to the class as a whole, spend a little time on the first part, the meaning of "Chicken Little Day." It could be in commemoration of the time in Columbus, Ohio, when the dam broke – but didn't; or it could be in honor of the faint-hearted who panicked when the "War of the Worlds" was broadcast on radio in 1938. As an ironic holiday, it has the virtue of our laughing at ourselves, something we do very seldom as a people.

Making up nicknames for the days of the week should be as entertaining as making up nicknames for holidays. There actually may be nicknames for Sunday, Monday, and the rest in addition to "Hump Day" for Wednesday. If you know of one, keep it to yourself until after your students have made their attempts. There are people who love to give nicknames to others (George W. Bush is reputed to be fond of nicknaming people), and you could have one or two in your class. Insist on nicknames that are in good taste and not cruel.

Following Through

Activities your students could engage in after finishing "Chicken Little Day" include:

• Determine which of the nicknames for the holidays are best among those invented by class members.

• Determine which of the nicknames for the days of the week are best among those invented by the students.

• Have a debate about whether people should or should not refer to a holiday with a nickname. Is there something sacred about a holiday (as the word originally suggested)?

• Have a debate as to whether we have too many holidays or not enough of them.

CHICKEN LITTLE DAY

1. Jerry received a letter from a friend last year that puzzled him when he stumbled across it the other day. Instead of a date, the heading had "Chicken Little Day." Jerry couldn't recall at what time of the year he had received the letter, but he thought that "Chicken Little Day" might have been used by his correspondent in place of the name of a holiday. He supposed it could be the same kind of nickname some give Thanksgiving, namely, "Turkey Day." What do you suppose the writer meant by "Chicken Little Day?"

2. In addition to "Turkey Day," there probably are a number of nicknames for each of our holidays. Can you come up with some original nicknames for these holidays?

   a. Halloween _____

   b. Independence Day _____

   c. Labor Day _____

   d. Thanksgiving _____

   e. Memorial Day _____

   f. President's Day _____

   g. Valentine's Day _____

   h. Columbus Day _____

3. Some people call Wednesday "Hump Day." Can you guess why? Give nicknames to the different days of the week.

   a. Sunday _____

   b. Monday _____

   c. Tuesday _____

   d. Wednesday _____

   e. Thursday _____

   f. Friday _____

   g. Saturday _____

Activity Matching Names with Businesses and Writing Riddles (45-50 minutes)
Activity Sheet "Can Abby Patch It?"

Introducing the Activity

This is a playful activity, and it should be entered into in that spirit. Therefore, you should administer it at a time when your students aren't too anxious or serious. You can say: **Here is an activity for you to play around with. I think you'll like it, especially at the end where you can make up riddles."**

Administering the Activity

This can be administered to the entire class or to individual students. Your students are to match people's names with businesses at the beginning of "Can Abby Patch It?" All of the surnames given are legitimate, even Klunk and Sick. (Some people are cursed with undesirable names!) Then, in the second section, your students are asked to supply names for businesses.

The last section ends with an invitation to write a riddle. Some of your students may feel too sophisticated to engage in riddling, but they should get swept along with the others if you are doing this as a class exercise and there is enthusiasm for it. You can make the enterprise more acceptable and appealing by offering your own favorite riddle. If they have never composed a riddle before, give your students plenty of time to succeed.

Following Through

Among the activities that might follow "Can Abby Patch It?" are these:

• Have your students put together a booklet of their riddles.

• With permission from the authors, insert two or three of the best riddles (perhaps determined by vote) in a student publication.

• Have your students examine the local telephone book for unusual business names. A rich source is found in the beauty salon section in the yellow pages. In one telephone book there are listed "Shear Pizzaz," "Shear Pleasure," Snip Hair Design," Mane Attraction," "Perfect Temptation," "Village Hairitage," "Heads Up Beauty Salon," and "Absolute Panache Hair Design Team." And that's just in one small town. Note the tendency to pun.

• Have your students make a list of unusual surnames that they find.

CAN ABBY PATCH IT?

1. Sometimes we become aware that the names of businesses are especially appropriate. The names of beauty parlors are particularly eye-catching. Shops such as Shear Delight, Mane Attraction, Northwest Hair Lines, and Hair Deposit are typical of the clever names that people in that line of work have used to attract customers. Very often the owners of busi- nesses like to identify what they do with their names. For instance, Irvin's Drugs, Vunk's Bicycle Shop, Burst's Candies, and Hiron's Drug Store are named for their proud owners. Some names are particularly well suited to be used in the certain businesses. What businesses should these people be in?

Hart _____   Hazzard _____

Green _____   Marble _____

Klunk _____   Deal _____

Trout _____   Steele _____

Ash _____   Roemer _____

Fix _____   Peel _____

Sick _____   Settle _____

2. As you know, many surnames derive from the occupation of the person who, in times past, did a certain kind of work; prominent examples are Smith, Skinner, Carpenter, Baker, Mason, and Taylor. What would be appropriate names for the following businesses? (For example, a marriage counselor could be Abigail Patchett.)

Landscaping

_____

Pharmacy

_____

Well Drilling

_____

Heating

_____

Bottling company

_____

Dentistry

_____

Bus Company

_____

Music Store

_____

Construction company

_____

Floral Company

_____

3. If you were to write a little verse about Abby, the marriage counselor, it might go like this:

A patcher of sails, I do much mending;

Marital voyages bound for the rocks

I try to keep from ending. What is my job?

Make up a riddle like the one above. Just write a three-line verse and then add, "What's my job?" You can experiment with your verse in the space below.

_____

_____

_____

_____

_____

ADDITIONAL ACTIVITIES FOR PRACTICING
HIGHLIGHTING THE ESSENCE

• An effective way for students to use the skill is for them to make up their own heraldic designs or coats of arms. The design should depict the most important characteristics of the student's family, so he must determine what the family's primary characteristic is and then the secondary ones when he designs his coat of arms.

• Have your students read this problem orally:

What is the basic characteristic that these events have in common?

A. being awarded a blue ribbon for the best pie at the fair

B. getting 12 strikes in 12 frames in bowling

C. reaching the summit of a 14,000' mountain

D. passing the road test for a driver's license examination

E. being granted a patent

• Have your students examine a conflict, such as a dispute between neighbors, countries, labor and management, and the like. They should analyze the situation and then list the factors or events that have caused the conflict. Then they should identify the basic source of disagreement. By doing so, they will have a better idea of an effective resolution of the conflict.

• Read one of Aesop's lesser known fables and ask your students to write the moral on a piece of paper. Collect the papers and discuss their answers.

Reference

Torrance, E. P. and H. T. Safter (1999). Making the Creative Leap Beyond. Buffalo, N.Y.: Creative Education Foundation Press.

"ADDING ON"

There are people whose strength is generating ideas but whose weakness is bringing those ideas to fruition. In this lesson, your students are asked to use their own ideas and to elaborate upon various stimuli. In "What's Happening?" they elaborate upon a scene, and so the emphasis is upon planning, extending, embroidering, and expanding the idea for the story and not upon originating it.

> **Thinking skills emphasized**
>
> - **elaborating**
> - being original
> - being sensitive, finding the problem
> - putting ideas into context
> - analyzing
> - making judgments
> - hypothesizing

In Torrance's (Torrance and Safter, 1990, 1999) theory of creative thinking, **elaboration** is the ability to develop, implement, work out plans, and/or add details for an idea or product. He cautions that spending too much time elaborating can be costly in terms of time, expense, and original thinking. In "Adding On," however, the germ of an idea for a story is given, but it is the development and flowering of the idea that matter.

Activity Taking a Scene and Making It into a Story (45-50 minutes and perhaps an additional class period) **Activity Sheet** "What's Happening?"

Preparing for the Activity

This activity can work well with lessons in writing and vocabulary (diction), especially as a follow-up of a lesson about adjectives. Probably more important than warming up your students for "What's Happening?" is the timing of administering it. It's hard to know when your students are in the mood to write a story, but you can usually tell when they are not. Choose a time when they are relatively calm and perhaps serious. Be sure to give them enough time to finish their stories. Some of your students will spend a bare minimum, of course, but a few comments or questions from you can encourage them to flesh out their ideas.

The five "story starters" are not sure-fire (is anything ever sure-fire in the classroom?). So you are urged to substitute your own scenes for those you feel won't be inspiring enough for your students.

Administering the Activity

It is important to have a positive atmosphere when administering an activity such as this one. As you are passing it out you might say: **I think you'll find a couple of exciting ideas for writing a story here. If you aren't able to finish your story, you'll have time to do so later on.**

Following Through

An effective way to provide both motivation and quality to the stories is to have your students pair off and read to one another. They will be honest and tactful with each other because each student is in the same boat. If any of your students are willing to share their stories, encourage them to do so; but you won't want to insist that all reveal their stories to the class.

Notes

WHAT'S HAPPENING?

Here are five brief scenes. Each is puzzling in its own way. Maybe you can explain what is happening and what will happen. Write a short story with one of the scenes as its starting point. Try to use descriptive words that are effective in getting across your mean- ing and the flavor of the story. Use <u>adjectives</u> that help the reader get a picture of the action – words that give humor, color, emotion, and detail to your story.

1. It was very cold. Fay looked past the muddy road on to the field. Then she gasped and leaned forward. She reached into her pocket and pulled out something.

   What did Fay see?

   What did she pull out of her pocket? Why do you think so?

   What happened next?

2. Henry squinted. He placed his hands at right angles to his brows to reduce the glare. Then he began running very hard over the snow-covered slope.

   What did Henry see? Why do you think so?

   Why did he run hard?

   What happened next?

3. Larry was coming to the top of the hill. He walked past the big tree. Two birds were singing noisily. Then he looked to his right. He saw something dark in the ground. It was a big hole. Something darted into the hole. Larry went over to the big hole and looked in.

   What did Larry see? Why do you think so?

   What darted into the hole?

   What happened next?

4. Lisa ran across the room, snapped off the television set, and then ran out of the room sobbing. The elderly man seated in front of the set slowly turned his head as she fled the room. He moved his fingers up and down the broad red-and-white suspenders that held up his spotless work pants and then lowered his chin on his chest.

Why was Lisa disturbed? How old is she?

Who is the old man? Is he related to Lisa?

Where did the scene take place? When did it take place?

What will happen next?

5. The musicians were enthusiastically playing the last chorus of a rollicking tune when suddenly one of the trumpeters put down his horn and scrambled off the bandstand. He grabbed one of the dancers by the arm and let out a cry of joy.

Why did the trumpet player rush down among the dancers and grasp one of them by the arm?

Why was the musician so happy?

What kind of dance hall were they in?

What kind of a person was the trumpeter?

What will happen next?

Choose one of the five scenes as the starting point for your story, which should be enriched by colorful descriptions and gripping action.

Alternate Activity Elaborating Upon an Incomplete Figure and Writing a Story (45-50 minutes) **Activity Sheet** "Your Sketch"

Introducing the Activity

The "warming-up" part of the activity is the type of activity which can be given to your students at almost any time. You may find that it serves particularly well as a change-of-pace from the regular routine. While the idea of inviting students to write stories about their imaginative drawings is not new, recent studies concerning creative thinking have revealed this to be an effective device for stimulating original writing. Teachers have known for many, many years that one of the best ways to motivate a student to write enthusiastically is to have him put something of himself in his work. This activity is predicated upon this principle: the student perceives the lines in his own way; he elaborates upon his drawing; then he develops his ideas about his creation; and, finally, he organizes his ideas into a story about his creation.

Roughly speaking, there are two ways in which this exercise and the ones to follow can be introduced to your students. One method is for you to be alert to the situations which occur in and out of the classroom that will allow you to introduce the activity naturally. An example of the "natural" kind of situation that would permit you to employ this activity meaningfully would be an occasion when someone has brought up the subject of how difficult it is for people to interpret "abstract" art.

The other way of introducing one of these exercises is to plan to introduce the exercise to your students at a particular time. If you believe that it is not necessary to set the stage too painstakingly, you might merely prepare your class for the activity by comparing structure in painting or sculpture with structure in literature. On the other hand, if you feel that there should be more preparation if the activity is to have some genuine connection with the class's ongoing activities, you might point out to them something ambiguous which can be found in a composition, textbook, or some other material in the room. A discussion of how the ambiguous object might be perceived would lead the class naturally into the initiating activity of "What Is It?" The extent to which you prepare the ground for the activity will depend upon many factors, such as the maturity of your class, the length of the class session, and the familiarity of your students with the type of material contained in the activity.

Administering the Activity

The drawing task was chosen to initiate "Your Sketch" in fiction writing because it should loosen up your students' imaginations and free them from some of the inhibiting factors that often stifle creative writing. As psychologists have shown, individuals perceive in a multitude of ways. The lines presented are not actually part of the outline of any particular shape, but your students will probably find enough stimulation in them to be able to produce interesting drawings.

The individuality with which we receive sense data is a source of richness and also a source of misunderstanding to us. A major purpose of these lessons is to help the student gain an appreciation of the diversity of human experience by making him aware of his own unique perceptions, thereby increasing his understanding of others. If you are able to prevent your students from broadcasting their interpretations of the lines when they first see this exercise, you should be presented with an amazing variety of drawings.

Through these lessons there is an emphasis upon having the student preserve his ideas in some form. The student must be shown that his ideas are worthwhile. One of the best ways of demonstrating that you value him as an individual is to provide him with opportunities for writing down his ideas.

If you would like to introduce or reinforce outlining skills, this activity will afford you an opportunity to point out the advantages of organizing a story in outline form. Although some successful mystery story writers are supposed to never know how their plots are resolved until they actually write the endings, it is a good policy to require young writers to think through their story ideas before they begin writing. It is not important that the object that the pupil has drawn be featured prominently in the story – it serves simply as a taking-off point in his thinking.

Following Through

We believe that the most powerful tool a teacher possesses is praise. If you can find the means to point out the excellences in each student's story, your students will be much more likely to become increasingly skillful in the difficult art of putting words together creatively. The method you choose for giving your approval will depend upon your interpretation of your relationship to the student and upon his emotional commitment in writing his story. You may well encourage different students in different ways – a detailed commentary on the story for some, a conference for others, oral readings, and so forth. What matters is your attitude toward the productions of your students, which is to say, the main factor in the teaching-learning situation is your attitude toward the individuals in your class.

Notes

"Your Sketch"

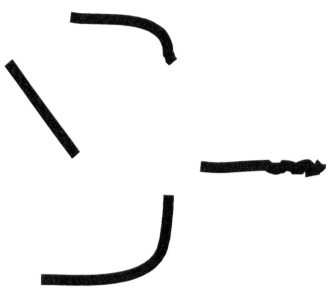

A. What do the lines above suggest to you?

It might help if you decide whether they represent something either alive or inanimate. It will also help you in seeing a more complete picture if you think of the lines as representing an object, an animal, a person, or a plant.

Now that you have done some thinking about the lines, draw some more lines and show what it really is. If you have some colored pencils or crayons, you might give it color, too.

B. Here are some questions that you should be able to answer about your creation above:
    1. Where would someone be most likely to see it?
    2. When would be the best time to see it?
    3. Are there any more like it anywhere?
    4. Can you describe its nature or some characteristics that are not obvious by just examining your picture?
    5. What, in your opinion, is the most interesting thing about your creation?
    6. Do you think anyone else would be interested in it? If so, show him or it or her to your classmates.

C. Now that you have done a good deal of thinking about your creation, write a story about it. (If it is not alive, you might write a story in which it is featured.) Remember to give your story a title, and don't forget to proofread the first draft before you write the second draft.

Extension

Activity Making up Designs out of Letters (40-50 minutes)
Materials pencils, pens, rulers, crayons (optional), colored chalk (optional)
Activity Sheet "Let's Go A-Lettering"

This is an activity that calls for individuality, and so it is best to have your students work independently. Since it calls for designs and not words, it is more properly an art activity. Your students should find it challenging.

References

Torrance, E. P. and H. T. Safter (1990). <u>The Incubation Model of Teaching</u>. Buffalo, N.Y.: Bearly Limited.

Torrance, E. P. and H. T. Safter (1999). <u>Making the Creative Leap Beyond</u>. Buffalo, N.Y.: Creative Education Foundation Press.

Notes

LET'S GO A-LETTERING

A. It's amusing to invent designs and logos, and in some cases it can even be profitable. Let's see what you can do with some simple designs. Putting two numbers or letters together can be effective. For example, here are two sevens and two As.

1. Select any three letters of the alphabet. Then take two of each letter and attach the pair together, in any way you like, to make a simple design.

2. Look at those three designs above and make three more of the same letters that are quite different.

3. Now elaborate upon the three designs above by adding lines, color, and texture to them.

B. Of the designs you have created, which one do you like best? Why?

_____

_____

_____

_____

If you wanted to use a similar design for a monogram or personal logo, could you do it?

Why don't you find out? If you are successful in creating a monogram or logo, you might want to use it in various ways – on clothing, papers, books, and so forth.

"OPEN MINDS"

Whenever there is a tendency on the part of your students to jump to conclusions or to give only superficial attention to material that should be carefully scrutinized, you can bring this behavior to their attention. Propaganda of various kinds is being fed to the public all of the time; and so when you note their uncritical acceptance of an exaggerated sales pitch, or a cliche, call your students on it. Examine it with them, allowing them to come forth with opinions as to the truth, wisdom, and propriety of the statement(s) in question.

Thinking skills emphasized

- **keeping open**
- being original
- analyzing
- making judgments
- hypothesizing

The principal skill to be called for in this lesson is keeping open. Investigators such as Rogers (1979), Moustakas (1967, 1996), and Parnes (1967, 1998) have long stressed the critical importance of **withholding judgment** and avoiding premature closure in creative thinking. Deferring judgment is a fundamental rule in brainstorming. Accordingly, keeping open, Torrance's seventh creative thinking skill, is an important one in any scheme for encouraging creative production.

Activity Reacting to Five Cartoons of Widely Differing Personalities (45-50 minutes)
Activity Sheet "Five Folks"

Introducing the Activity

You might be rather casual when you introduce "Five Folks." It consists of five cartoon figures and a series of questions about them. The questions are designed to bring out the point that appearances are often deceiving. One can't really tell much about the character and tastes of people merely by glancing at them, but we often do just that. Simply say to your students when you hand out "Five Folks": **Here are cartoons of five people. If they were real people, what could you tell about them?**

Administering the Activity

For this lesson, it is probably wise to eliminate any kind of warmup. The idea is to allow your students to jump to conclusions and to reveal their prejudices before engaging in a serious discussion of the cartoon characters. After they have individually finished answering the questions, permit them to discuss their reactions with one another. Then lead the discussion without offering much in the way of comment. Allow your students to express any reactions they have to the five individuals. If there are any sharp differences of opinion, so much the better. After all, there are no "right" responses to the questions that are posed.

Following Through

To bring to light the hidden biases and prejudices that everyone has, you might play several highly contrasting kinds of music on a CD player. Choose some selections that are unfamiliar to your students (electronic music, perhaps a madrigal or a wind septet, a folk song from a remote corner of the world, or any others that would be quite unfamiliar) and a few that are all too familiar to them.

Have them rank the selections according to how they perceive them as "good" music. They should come to the generalization that being unfamiliar with something often leads us to dislike it, fear it, or be suspicious of it. This idea makes a good analogue to our behavior towards strange people.

Notes

FIVE FOLKS

Here are five people.

Which one doesn't wear socks?

Why do you think so?

Which one, in your opinion, likes to play checkers?

Why do you think so?

Extensions

Materials pencils, colored chalk, crayons

Activity Sheet "What Is It?"

Introducing the Activity

This activity is offered in the hope that your students can readily see that perceptions differ from person to person. One prominent educator sees the lines as indicating a Scotch terrier; the author usually sees a dolphin, and his wife sees an elephant. The individuality with which we receive sense data is a source of richness and also a source of misunderstanding for us.

You might use a verbal example to illustrate the differing interpretations people make about words before administering "What Is It?" Ambiguity is one of the great problems with letter writing and other forms of personal communication. Write: "Such a momentous week – we will be forever changed" on the chalkboard and ask for interpretations of the sentence.

Administering the Activity

To further the idea of your students' being open in their perceptions and judgments, hand out the incomplete figure presented in "What Is It?" Again, you needn't say much to your students before passing out the sheet of paper. You might simply say: **What can you make of this? If you'd like to add some lines and color to it after you've answered the questions, you may.**

As in "Five Folks," there are no right or wrong answers. Some students take comfort in the fact that they are in the majority in making the lines into an elephant, and that is only natural. However, you should emphasize the significance of the questions about the figure when it is rotated. Do your students get an entirely different idea when the figure is rotated or inverted?

Following Through

At the end of the activity your students are invited to begin working on their favorite activities. They are only invited to sketch out their plans, however. The actual carrying out of those plans, insofar as they relate to the classroom or to your curricular offerings, is left up to you and your students.

WHAT IS IT?

1. What does this look like to you?

Using the lines above, make whatever kind of an object you care to make. You may use additional lines if you wish – as many as you would like. When you have completed your drawing, color it.

2. Make up a story that features your object in some way. It can be any kind of story you'd like it to be. Be sure to give your story a title.

3. How valuable is your imagination? Do you think it is as valuable as your sense of humor? Or are these two "senses" related?

_____

_____

_____

_____

What activity requires more of your imagination than anything else you do?

_____

_____

_____

Think about starting in on one of your favorite imaginative activities now! You can jot down your plans in the space below.

_____

_____

_____

_____

_____

_____

_____

Activity Sheet "A Matter of Judgment" (45-50 minutes)

Introducing the Activity

This activity has the appearance of being a typical true or false exercise at its outset. It is quite possible that it won't grab your students' attention and interest for that reason. Therefore, if you choose to follow up "Five Folks" and "What Is It?" with "A Matter of Judgment," it will be wise to offer a few remarks about the power of the printed word and the unsubstantiated rumor. You might also say something like this: **When we are confronted with a problem, in spite of the natural tendency to rely upon reactions that seemed appropriate in the past, it is often wise not to jump to any conclusions. If we resist our impulse to reduce tension and offer a quick solution or conclusion and instead survey the situation and bring to bear any ideas that might illuminate the problem, we can often come up with satisfying solutions. Let's see how you do with these propositions.**

Administering the Activity

As we say, the individual should resist the urge to make premature closure; instead, by enlisting a variety of physical and mental resources, he or she can promote the incubation process, and a better solution can then be achieved. Keeping open means allowing one thing to lead to another in a natural way. Again, because of predispositions and preconceptions we tend to force certain actions when they may not be appropriate. When thinking creatively, we must get off the beaten track now and then and be prepared to break away. Rigidity of thinking can lead to predictable, outmoded behavior. On the other hand, keeping open can take us down delightful pathways.

Following Through

Among the activities you might administer to your students after they have completed "A Matter of Judgment" are these:

• Have a general discussion of their attempts at making up an exercise similar to "A Matter of Judgment." Encourage those who are willing to try out a few items on the class. This inevitably will lead to a debate about fact versus opinion or the appropriateness of words when making statements.

• As an additional excursion into the problems of the veracity of printed words, you can consider erroneous reports that get transmitted in the media, propaganda, and the role of facts in historical fiction.

• Discuss the differences between the second and third items in "A Matter of Judgment." The second statement about the fact that some birds do not build nests is verifiable by consulting authorities about birds; whereas the statement about the children being punished because Nancy was cheating is a different kind of proposition and is not verifiable. The key word is should (be punished). "Should" is almost always a matter of opinion.

A MATTER OF JUDGMENT

1. We make judgments about the quality, character, and suitability of people and things everyday. Unfortunately, many of our judgments are made without much reflection; we don't bother to check into the essential nature of information concerning the person, object, process, organization, or whatever might be the subject of our judgment. In this exercise, reflect about the elements of the statement before you make a decision as to its soundness.

1. Place an **L** to the left of the statements below which you believe to be **logical**. Place an **I** to the left of those statements which you think are **illogical** or **invalid**. Be careful to understand the terms of each statement before you make a decision. If you have any difficulty with the words, look them up in your dictionary. Give a brief explanation of your answer for each statement.

_____ A. First, the farmer planted corn seed; then he shucked the corn; and finally he harvested the corn crop.

_____ B. Some birds do not build nests.

_____ C. Since Nancy was discovered to be cheating during the test, all of the children in the class should be punished.

_____ D. Bill was the logical choice for the office of president because the other two candidates were girls.

_____ E. After Mr. Jennings lost his voice, he was forced to shout his directions through a megaphone.

_____ F. General Armstrong's forces marched rapidly to the south in pursuit of the enemy, which had retreated in disorder to the north.

_____ G. Blinded by the terrible dust storm, Mrs. Nelson crouched behind a rock and waited until she saw her husband's signal.

2. Write an exercise like this one. Just think of several sentences which are logical and some which have an element of contradiction or implausibility. Mix them together, and then try to stump your friends.

3. How successful were you in making up an exercise in logical thinking? If you weren't too successful, can you figure out why? Did you perhaps find that you hadn't seen all of the implications of your own statements? What did you learn from devising your own logical thinking exercise?

"THE ROLE OF EMOTIONS"

The **role of emotions in learning** has gained increasing prominence in the ways that educators analyze the teaching-learning process. Your students will be given several opportunities in this lesson to appreciate their own emotions and also the emotions of others.

Thinking skills emphasized

- **being aware of emotions**
- being sensitive, finding the problem
- being original
- visualizing richly and colorfully
- letting humor flow
- analyzing
- making judgments

To the surprise of many, Edward de Bono (1995) has stated that emotions are more important than anything else in thinking. He believes that emotions come first and that thinking is used to support and back up an individual's emotions. Safter and Crammond (1987) found that those children who responded empathically to the emotional distress of others scored higher on tests measuring creative behavior.

Activity Describing Embarrassing Moments (30-45 minutes)
Activity Sheet "Describe It in Detail"

Introducing the Activity

Note: If there's recently been an embarrassing incident in your classroom and the students involved are uncomfortable about it, move to another lesson and come back to this one later.

Introduce the activity by saying something like the following: **All of us have embar-rassing experiences from time to time. No one likes to be embarrassed! In this activity, you'll look at, imagine, and describe six awkward or uncomfortable situations.**
Distribute the activity sheet. Individually or in small groups, have students look at each situation and describe what's asked for in their own words. To help students get started, you might invite one or two to suggest words to describe the look on the woman's face in the first situation. Or, you might suggest a few expressive descriptors such as horrified, pained, or wickedly gleeful. Discuss the possible physical signs of embarrassment (such as downcast eyes or flushing). Allow 5-10 minutes for students to write on their own. Then have groups of 2-4

students compare what they wrote and enact several of the situations, emphasizing in their role playing the aspect of the scene the activity sheet focuses on. Challenge group members to think of other ways of describing the situations, based on the role plays. Allow about 10 minutes for groups to do this. Bring the class together and ask for volunteers to read some of the descriptions they wrote. Discuss questions such as the following:

• What are some other words to describe how the woman might look and feel?

• Why would the flight attendant look like that?

• Why was the football player embarrassed?

• How else might the police officer show her feelings about the parking ticket?

• How could you tell the diner was embarrassed about losing his contact lens? Would any person who lost a contact lens in a bowl of soup feel embarrassed about it? Explain your answer.

• How did the student feel after falling in front of the others? Would you have felt and acted the same way if this had happened to you? Why or why not?

• What feelings go along with embarrassment?

• How does it feel to watch someone do something embarrassing? What are some ways we react when someone else is embarrassed?

• When is embarrassment funny? When isn't it funny? How do you decide that?

Allow 10-15 minutes for discussion.

Following Through

Activities to follow "Describe It in Detail" include:

• You can invite your students to write about their reactions to witnessing an embarrassing scene and then have a discussion about ways to prevent or avoid being embarrassed.

• Your students might create short radio spots where the speaker talks on topics such as "Me? Embarrassed? No way!" or "If you think that's embarrassing, you should have seen . . ."

• You might have groups create headlines and news stories about embarrassing moments different kinds of media, such as The National Inquirer, New York Times, a late-night TV show, a Web 'Zine, etc.

DESCRIBE IT IN DETAIL

Write one or more descriptions for each of the following embarrassing moments. Your description can be funny or serious – be as creative as you'd like! If you need more room to write, use the back of this form or attach a sheet of notebook paper.

1. A woman has just finished her first up-close conversation with an important client. She excuses herself to go to the restroom. There, she sees in the mirror that she has a huge piece of spinach stuck to her front tooth. Write about the expression on the woman's face using as many descriptive words as possible:

_____

_____

_____

_____

2. A flight attendant has just spilled a large glass of soda on the lap of an extremely fussy first-class passenger. Describe the flight attendant's facial and body expressions:

_____

_____

_____

_____

3. A star varsity football player is bowling with classmates. He knows everyone expects him to be as skilled at bowling as he is at running for touchdowns. With all eyes watching, he bowls a gutter ball. Describe how he feels:

_____

_____

_____

_____

4. A police officer returns to her car after a longer-than-expected coffee break and finds a parking ticket on her windshield. Describe her emotions:

_____

_____

_____

_____

5. A diner in a restaurant has just lost his contact lens in his soup. He doesn't want to draw attention to himself, but he needs to find the contact. Describe his actions:

_____

_____

_____

_____

6. A student has just pushed and shoved to get to the front of a group of kids hurrying to get on the bus. The student slips on a patch of ice and lands in front of several of the kids. Describe what the student does and says next:

_____

_____

_____

_____

Extensions

Allow 5-15 minutes in class for any of the following activities, assign them as homework, or continue them in another class period:

• Have students write more elaborate descriptions or describe what happens next for incidents in "Describe It in Detail."

• Have students work in small groups to suggest creative solutions to help the embarrassed person. Invite groups to role play their ideas for the large group.

• Ask students to make up other embarrassing situations and write sentences or paragraphs describing aspects of the situations such as how the people felt, how they showed their feelings, or how they behaved in the situations.

• Have students discuss or write about one of the scenarios from the other person's or a witness's point of view.

• Brainstorm similes that show how embarrassed someone is. (Example: "The sweat streamed down his neck like rain on a windshield.")

Activity Describing the Feelings That Result in Surprising Events (30-45 minutes)
Activity Sheet "How Would You Feel?"

Introducing the Activity

Before handing out "How Would You Feel?" make a few remarks about surprises. You might say: **Do you like surprises? Yes, it depends upon what kind they are, doesn't it? In this activity you are to imagine that you have seven unusual things happen to you. As you read about each situation, imagine that it really happens to you and give an honest reaction.**

Administering the Activity

There is an element of humor in some of the situations described in the activity, and your students should respond accordingly without being silly. The main idea is to probe your students about how they deal with their emotions when the unexpected happens. It's at those times, when our guard is down, that we expose our true natures.

You should substitute situations that you consider more appropriate for your students for any of those given.

After your students have reacted in writing to the seven situations, a class discussion could prove enlightening.

The short story exercise at the end is optional, but it might prove to be a very successful writing activity if "How Would You Feel?" generates some genuine interest.

Following Through

We often laugh when someone falls down or makes a mistake. What is there in the situation that makes us laugh at someone's discomfort? Why do we think it's funny when someone else is embarrassed? You can discuss this paradox with your class if they seem open to inquiring into what is really a peculiarity of mankind.

References

De Bono, E. (1995). Mind Power. New York: Dorling Kindersky.

Safter, H. T. and H. Crammond (November 1987). "Children who push, children who pat – results of a study in empathy in preschool children." National Association for Gifted Children, Washington D.C.

Notes

HOW WOULD YOU FEEL?

There are many occasions when something happens that we couldn't possibly have foreseen. Sometimes those occasions are so peculiar we hardly know how to act. But those experiences can definitely cause us to have certain emotions. Here are seven surprises that you probably haven't had, but people have had them or ones like them.

1. Someone comes up and congratulates you on your victory in an election. But you've never even been nominated. Your reaction:

_____

_____

_____

2. You fall off a bicycle and a news photographer who happened to be nearby takes your picture. The next day the newspaper prints it under the heading, "Young person litters the sidewalk." Your reaction:

_____

_____

_____

3. You have just hit a home run to win a ball game. A teammate comes up to you and criticizes you for wearing dirty socks. Your reaction:

_____

_____

_____

4. You are asked for the first time to babysit for the neighbors. Everything goes very well until they come home, whereupon their five-year-old begins to cry furiously. Your reaction:

_____

_____

_____

5. Your dog has just won a prize in a big show for dogs of all breeds. As you lead him away from the award stand, he nips you on the ankle.
Your reaction:

_____

_____

_____

6. You think you have done rather poorly on a test. The teacher hands back the test papers and yours has an "A" on it. Your reaction:

_____

_____

_____

7. You have just met someone, and he keeps calling you "Robin." Your name isn't "Robin." Finally, after the 13th or 14th time of being called "Robin," you correct him. He just says, "That's okay. I never liked the name 'Robin' anyway." Your reaction:

_____

_____

_____

Have you had an experience similar to one of those above? What happened? How did you feel when it happened? Write about your experience – or imagine one – and put it into the form of a short, short story. You can use the space below for jotting down your ideas for the story.

"IN THE PROPER PLACE AND TIME"

There are a lot of empty places to be filled in our lives. We plug in most with what we have used before, but there are a number of situations in which we have to use both our knowledge and our imagination to fill in the gaps.

Thinking skills emphasized

- **putting ideas into context**
- being sensitive, finding the problem
- letting humor flow
- analyzing
- making judgments
- hypothesizing

Buckminster Fuller (1992) maintained that any genuinely creative idea requires the individual to put things in **context**. He believed that the mind has the innate ability to fit what it's not looking for into the context of an individual's concepts. When you think about it, it is this remarkable ability that has led to progress throughout history.

Activity Explaining Why Gaps Should and Should Not Be Filled (45-50 minutes)
Activity Sheet "Gaps"

Introducing the Activity

This activity is comprised of a rather lengthy introduction, an activity in which your students are to explain why they would not want to fill 10 gaps of various kinds, another section in which they are to name two gaps that they would like filled and two they would not like to see filled, and a serious question about what gap they would like to have filled most of all. As you can readily see, your students are hit from all angles with the concept.

Preparing for the Activity

A gap is like a hole – something is missing. Teachers are concerned with gaps of knowledge; football coaches are concerned with gaps in a line; actors are sometimes concerned about gaps between their front teeth; and overweight people are concerned about gaps in their clothing (although the word "gaposis" isn't found in advertising any longer). If you would like to lead into this unit with a few words or an object or two, you can find any number of gaps to illustrate the concept. Costa (1981) believes that before students should be asked to think, they should have a series of sense experiences. We provide a number of examples of gaps in the introduction, but you may also want to prepare your students for the activity by having them actually doing some looking and touching, or even tasting and smelling.

Administering the Activity

If you decide simply to say a few words and present "Gaps" to your students without a buildup, the written introduction will probably be adequate for warming them up. Undoubtedly, however, a bunch of words on a piece of paper is not as effective as their seeing a couple of teeth missing from a comb, or noting an empty seat in the room, or hearing someone tell a joke and leave out an important part.

After the concept has been introduced, then the activity should be completed by your students individually. You may want to know how they respond to the final question, however, and a most productive session could grow out of their choices of naming the "most serious gaps" they have. Of course, some of these gaps may be of a highly personal nature, and you will welcome only the responses of students who are eager to share their ideas and feelings.

Following Through

Activities that could follow the successful completion of "Gaps" include:

• Have volunteers tell a story and leave out a vital part. (What did she leave out?)

• Have volunteers give the directions for getting from their homes to school, leaving out an important part. (What part did she leave out?)

• For homework, give the class the assignment of finding gaps in the authorized biography of a person such as Abraham Lincoln, Elvis Presley, George W. Bush, Charles Dickens, Albert Einstein, Maya Angelou, or a person your class has been studying.

• For homework, have the class search for gaps or omissions in their family trees (back through three generations).

Notes

GAPS

Sometimes a young person tries to recite the alphabet and comes up with something like this:

"A, B, C, F, G, H, I, M . . . "

The list of letters is incomplete, and the recitation sounds a little strange and humorous to an adult who might be listening. One way of regarding the child's list is to say that there are **gaps** in it.

Similarly, there can be gaps in our knowledge of geography, history, or mathematics. In the case of the last-named discipline, a gap can mean that the individual fails to understand an equation or formula or can't solve a problem. With regard to a gap in the individual's knowledge of geography, he or she can get lost, fail to understand the significance of an important development, or become confused by a newspaper or television news report.

The fact of the matter is, however, that all of us have countless gaps in our knowledge. We're in the business of filling in gaps all of the time. There are any number of times during an ordinary day when you try to fill a gap by learning what a good friend did over the weekend, by finding out the name of a new song you heard for the first time, by looking up a strange word in the dictionary, and the like.

Here are 10 gaps or voids that you would probably want to fill: the inside of your shoes in the morning, an empty stomach, an empty gas tank, four spaces for a word in a crossword puzzle, an empty purse, the missing ingredient in a recipe for a cake, a space in a jigsaw puzzle, a grocery sack, a fill-in answer to a test item in class, and the place of a good friend who has moved to another state. When would you NOT want to fill those particular gaps? Explain why.

1. inside of your shoes in the morning

_____

2. an empty stomach

_____

3. an empty gas tank

_____

4. four spaces for a word in a crossword puzzle

_____

5. an empty purse

_____

6. the missing ingredient in a recipe for a cake

_____

7. a space in a jigsaw puzzle

_____

8. a grocery sack

_____

9. a fill-in answer to a test item in class

_____

10. the place of a good friend who has moved to another state

_____

There are times when we do want to fill in a gap and others when we don't. For example, you might want to put in a picket that is missing in a fence if you want to keep a dog inside a yard, or you might want to leave the gap if that is the way a dog or cat usually leaves and returns to the house. Also, there are times when you want to plug the nostrils of your nose to keep out noxious fumes or to stop water from coming into your head when you are swimming, but there is mostly an urge to breathe and you take medicine so that the nasal passages are open. Name at least two other gaps that you'd both want filled and not filled.

1. _____

2. _____

Which is the most serious gap that you have? Tell why you think so. What criteria are you using to determine that it is your most serious gap?

_____

_____

_____

_____

Alternate Activity Finding the Missing Facts in Two Stories and Writing a Mystery Story (50 minutes and perhaps a second class period)
Activity Sheet "What's Missing?"

Introducing the Activity

Some classes are more fond of solving puzzles than others. However, judging from the number of crossword puzzles and mystery story fans in our country, the chances are good that you have several students who like to solve puzzles. "What's Missing?" can be introduced on almost any occasion when you are looking for a change of pace from the more routine tasks in your program. If your students have been doing any hypothesizing about why an event has taken place, or if they have been perplexed by someone's behavior, the lesson can be brought in naturally and effectively.

Administering the Activity

Since there is a large amount of explanatory material that precedes the warming-up portion of "What's Missing?" it may be well for you to read the directions aloud with your students or have one of them do the reading. Very often teachers discover that their students have not bothered to read the directions for an activity. This is particularly vexing when the directions are essential for the proper execution of the activity. The idea of the warming-up part is to cause your students to do some detective work. Their sleuthing will be mainly concerned with formulating hypotheses on the basis of a limited number of facts. Because there are only a few facts in each situation, the student is able to allow her imagination to range freely. If some of the ideas produced by your students appear to be foolish or far-fetched but honestly conceived, give them respect. One of the greatest inhibitors of creative thinking is the fear of being ridiculed.

The writing assignment itself can be adapted and modified to suit whatever purposes you have in using the activity. Since young people are apt to enjoy writing mystery stories, that particular form was chosen. However, there is nothing sacred about any part of this activity or any of the others in this book.

Following Through

Inasmuch as your students will probably be writing mystery stories as an outcome of the warming-up activity, you might read their productions, and then pick one or two of the more suspenseful and have them read to the class. If you and your students think it is a good idea, the reader might stop before the mystery is solved and ask the class for their ideas about how it ends. This will serve three purposes: first, it will provide the authors with some recognition (and excellent stories should receive recognition); second, it will give your students practice in hypothesis-making, an important part of the creative process; and, third, it will give your students practice in reading aloud and listening attentively. When the lesson is completed, you should have several opportunities to notice whether your students have become more skillful in exploring the possibilities and seeing causal relationships. You might also use this activity to make your students more sensitively aware of causal relationships in their own behavior.

WHAT'S MISSING?

This is an activity that requires you to use your imagination in trying to figure out why a certain event has taken place. An important fact has been left out of each of the anecdotes which follow. Your job is to come up with a fact that will account for things turning out as they do. Let's look at this story to see what you are supposed to do:

Mary went to town on a bus one Saturday to do some shopping. She got off the bus at a busy corner and walked into a large department store. She decided to take an elevator to the second floor and look at some hats. After trying on several hats, she started for an elevator whose doors were just opening. When Mary was about to step into the elevator, a woman ran toward her and shouted, "Stop!"

What fact has been omitted in this anecdote which would explain the woman's behavior?

A number of different facts might be inserted into this story which would explain why the woman wanted Mary to stop. You might have thought of these possibilities already:
(a) Mary forgot to pay for the hat on her head; (b) she had put another woman's hat on by mistake; or (c) she dropped her purse and the woman was rushing to return it before the elevator doors closed. See if you can come up with the missing fact in the following anecdotes.

1. *Jerry drove his car to the lake one day when he felt like swimming. He parked his car by the side of the lake, got out of the car, and jumped into the water. After about 10 minutes he came out of the water. Just as he reached into his car for a towel, a policeman told him he was under arrest.*

Think of as many facts as you can that might have been left out of this story that would account for the policeman's action.

2. *Amelia and her dog went down a pathway in the country on a sunny spring day. Two birds twittered in an apple tree. A breeze stirred the branches of the tree, and several blossoms fell to the ground. Suddenly a rabbit darted across the path in front of Amelia and her dog. Without pausing, Amelia and her dog proceeded down the path.*

Why didn't Amelia's dog chase the rabbit? What are some of the important facts that might have been omitted from this anecdote that would explain the dog's behavior?

Extensions

Activity Reading a Story and Finding a Single Word to Identify What the Story Is About (15-30 minutes) **Activity Sheet** "Pogo"

Introducing the Activity

Since "Pogo" is a kind of game, you can sandwich it in between weightier language arts lessons at a time when your students deserve a change of pace. You might say: **Here is a puzzle for you this afternoon. It looks easy, but it's really not. When you can come up with just one word for "Pogo," you'll have solved the puzzle.**

Administering the Activity

The idea of "Pogo" is simple: a story is told about "Pogo," but its identity isn't given. All the student has to do is find a word that will substitute for "Pogo" many times in the story. This activity works best if administered to students individually.

It very well might be that "Pogo" will produce a good deal of frustration among your students. One word has to fit in all of these sentences. On the other hand, the unmotivated student may just find some word – any word – to get the exercise over, and not care much whether he has made a good selection. In general, you will have to encourage those who are less diligent. Try it yourself first.

Following Through

If you have time to follow up "Pogo," these are activities that might induce some learning:

• Have your students guess the number of times "Pogo" appeared in the activity sheet. (there are 22, including the title.)

• Ask them when is the best time to: sew on a button (Why?), wash a dog (Why?), take a walk (Why?), barbecue a chicken (Why?), learn a magic trick (Why?), paint a picture (Why?), play a computer game (Why?), talk to a cat (Why?), watch fireflies (Why?).

• Ask them where is the best place to: listen to the rain (Why?), swim (Why?), count your money (Why?), confide a secret (Why?), hold a political rally (Why?), announce a scientific breakthrough (Why?), eat a juicy hamburger (Why?).

• Give them this mystery: **When she reached the sidewalk, Carla suddenly stopped. Then she looked at the coins in her purse. Quickly, she ran back inside the store to the counter and said to the clerk, "Here is your quarter." Why did Carla go back into the store and give the clerk a quarter? What do you think the clerk said to Carla?**

94

POGO

This activity was designed to have you play around with words, something you've been doing ever since you were an infant. It's not a serious activity, but you may find it quite challenging.

Every time you see the word "POGO," change it to another word. The word should be the same each time.

Things were always like that in POGO. People didn't seem to behave as other people did. Most of the time, when one person would ask another a question, the answer was more likely to be a comment about POGO. Fathers would teach their sons how to POGO as soon as they could walk. Mothers would take their young daughters downtown to go shopping and then POGO instead. The biggest day of the year was the POGO celebration.

The one thing everyone was good at was POGO. They would POGO at the slightest opportunity. If there were a gathering of any kind, people would POGO. It was not only a craze; POGO was a prominent part of the personality of all the inhabitants of POGO. In fact, if anyone saw a person from POGO in another place, the first thing the person would be asked is, "Oh, you're from POGO – why do you POGO so much?"

The only drawback to this obsession with POGO in POGO was that people were reluctant to move there if they didn't POGO. So if anyone moved away or died and left a house vacant, you could be sure the new occupants could POGO. In that manner, POGO never changed much over the years. It was POGO in the past, and it always would be POGO.

Extensions

After your students have found a word to substitute for "Pogo," they can:

- draw what it is;

- pantomime what it is and have others guess what they think it is from watching the pantomime;

- continue the story; or

- write a song about it.

Activity Answering Six Questions about the Importance of Listening (25-30 minutes)
Activity Sheet "Popular Listening"

The idea to be put into various contexts in this activity is: some listening may not make you popular, but intelligent listening can be useful and valuable to anyone. In general, people who are good listeners <u>are</u> popular. In all honesty, however, it must be admitted that highly creative individuals are often unpopular.

Notes

POPULAR LISTENING

A teacher was being like a wise uncle when he gave this advice: "The individual who listens intelligently and gives the other person full attention has gone a long way toward popularity."

In addition to listening intelligently, there are many kinds of listening. Half-listening to a bore, full-attention listening when you are really interested, listening for sounds when driving or when alone in a house, listening to directions, and listening to music are just a few. What about listening attentively to a lecture? With whom does that make you popular?

Does listening to music on the radio make you popular at home? Why or why not?

_____

_____

_____

Does listening carefully to an argument between two friends make you popular? Why or why not? If so, with whom?

_____

_____

_____

Does listening to crickets at night make you popular? How <u>could</u> it make you popular?

_____

_____

_____

_____

Could listening – actually overhearing – a conversation between two adult relatives make you popular with anyone? How?

_____

_____

_____

Could listening to young children talk while playing on a playground make you popular? How could that kind of listening make you popular?

_____

_____

_____

Could listening to a symphony orchestra in a large hall make you popular? How and with whom?

_____

_____

_____

What can you gather from your answers to these questions?

_____

_____

_____

_____

_____

Activity Discussing "Free Zones" in Our Society (45-50 minutes)
Materials Sign (such as "Drug-Free Zone" or "Nuclear-Free Zone")

Topic: A "Free Society"

An alternate activity, stressing reflective speaking and listening instead of writing, would be to have a discussion of "free zones." You can bring to class a sign, such as one that reads "Nuclear-Free Zone," and ask the students to comment on it. You might say: **What legal right do citizens have for establishing such a zone?**

When students have examined the nuclear-free zone issue against a backdrop of constitutional rights, ask what other citizen action movements have emerged in recent times for establishing "free zones." After student feedback, you can discuss basic constitutional rights, emphasizing the preamble ("for the people, of the people, by the people"). If the discussion is lively and your students are interested, a special interest group might evolve that could be given the opportunity to campaign in the school for their "free zone." The more unusual the "free zone" the better to demonstrate that within the framework of law individual and group rights can be upheld.

References

Costa, A. L. (October 1981). "Teaching for Intelligent Behavior." Educational Leadership: 1 (39, 29-31.

Fuller, R. B. (1992). Cosmography: A Posthumous Scenario for the Future of Humanity. New York: Macmillan.

Notes

"PUTTING IT ALL TOGETHER"

One of the joys of life is putting things together. Whether it is a jigsaw puzzle, a delicious dish, or house, we love to see it all come together right. In this lesson your students will have an opportunity to combine several things creatively.

> **Thinking skills emphasized**
>
> - **combining and synthesizing**
> - being original
> - putting ideas into context
> - analyzing
> - making judgments

The painter, engineer, chemist, and chef all make their livings by putting things together. **Combining ideas and elements** is the essence of what they do. The trick is in how they are combined. Parnes (1975) believes that success in creative thinking is accompanied by the "aha" or "Eureka" experience, combining the fresh association of facts, ideas, and elements into a meaningful new configuration.

Activity Putting Elements Together in Writing a Story (45-50 minutes)
Materials biscuits (optional)
Activity Sheet "Chemical Writing"

Introducing the Activity

Before passing out "Chemical Writing" make a few remarks about the art of cooking. Most of your students will have attempted to cook something, if only a batch of cookies, and so they will be able to recall readily when their cooking was successful and when it wasn't very good. You could bake two biscuits for demonstration - one with too much salt and the other with too much baking soda. The ingredients must be in the right proportions, or the dish will be spoiled. The same is true of writing. When writers put too much description in their narration, for example, they often turn off their readers, who either don't finish reading the material or avoid reading that writer again. In this activity it is important that your students combine the elements of description, dialogue, characterization, and action in the correct proportions.

Administering the Activity

This activity is designed for the individual student. It is the kind that the less enthusiastic writer may welcome because she can simply put the elements together and the plot should appear, more or less, before her eyes. However, the work isn't done, of course, and it isn't quite as easy as a story starter exercise is to write.

Following Through

If some of the stories that are generated please your students, they can then go to the trouble of putting them in a form that can easily be read and understood by their classmates. There is no avoiding the fact that writing entails work; and correcting, revising, and writing second and third drafts doesn't appeal to many students.

Nevertheless, they can understand the necessity of all that effort if they read a classmate's story and have problems with the handwriting (if it isn't done on a word processor), punctuation, spelling, organization, and the other mechanics of writing.

This activity will give you an opportunity to review the principles of good story writing. You can ask these questions of your students after they have written their first drafts:

Interest

- Is the idea of your story interesting enough for others to want to read it?
- Is your title catchy or sufficiently intriguing?
- Are your characters interesting?
- If you chose to make the setting a prominent element, was it suitable for your plot?

Organization

- Is your story logically organized?
- If it is organized chronologically, are scenes sequenced so that readers aren't confused?
- Is there a climax to your story following a proper buildup?

Details

- Did you give enough information about your characters to make them seem believable?
- Did you provide your readers with enough information about the setting so that a picture emerges in their minds?
- Did you put enough detail in your story to make it entertaining without the story becoming too lengthy or boring?
- Do your sentences have variety?

Form
- Is your story in a form that can be easily read?

CHEMICAL WRITING

Just as a chemist takes certain ingredients and adds them to other ingredients, a writer puts together events and conditions in order to come up with a lively, entertaining story. Let's make a scientific writer out of you by having you (1) find two items that go together, (2) mix them together, and (3) add other items (that is, condition, activity, or event), and then (4) come up with a story.

1. This is the first step: look over this list of items and find two which, as a pair, interest you when you think about them together.

charcoal	ham	cream	shoes	train	policeman
spider	soap	book	wallet	shark	fence
cliff	swing	bobcat	comb	bear	light switch
egg	star	pony	hatchet	mother	newspaper
magazine	billboard	rifle	lamp	hair net	boy
knife	kitten	girl	tramp	banker	grandfather
missionary	ball	horn	hairdresser		

Which two items interest you when they are paired? _____

Think about the two items you have picked. Why do they interest you when you think of them together?

2. Now, add an activity or an event or a condition to the two things you have chosen. Here are some activities, events, and conditions to choose from. You may also use any that you can think of that are not on these lists.

Event

eclipse	earthquake	landslide	storm	fracture
theft	fire	puncture	nightmare	wedding
rescue	crash	flood	explosion	

Activity

picnic	pursuit	trip	awakening	parade
synthesis	haircut	argument	wandering	conversation
playing a game	whistling	screeching	writing a letter	

Condition

severe cold	desolation	confusion	searing heat	luminescence
panic	collapse	flat	closed	asleep
floating	open	very wet	very dry	

3. The last step in this exercise of word chemistry is to put all of the elements together and write a story. Often writers find that their plots are practically developed when they have put together the critical elements of their story - the characters, the special incidents, and the themes. We'll leave the themes for you to devise, but you should have enough leads about the other important elements to compose a good story. You can start now by writing down the several elements and then sketching a trial plot in the space below.

the pair of items: _____ and _____

the event: _____

the activity: _____

the condition: _____

(your title) _____

_____

_____

_____

_____

_____

_____

_____

Extensions

Activity Combining Sentence Parts into Complete Sentences and Drawing a Cartoon with One of the Sentences as the Caption (45-50 minutes)
Materials pencils, crayons, colored chalk, felt pens
Activity Sheet "Grandmothers and Traffic Cops"

Introducing the Activity

Tell your class that you have a puzzle for them and that they are to work independently. As you distribute the activity sheet you might say: You should have some fun making sentences out of these groups of words. It's easy to come up with some funny ones, too. Don't worry too much about getting them together as they were originally written.

Administering the Activity

The activity starts with a game of recombining eight sentences that have been broken up into three parts. There are plenty of clues (capital letters, clauses, phrases), and so every student should be able to complete the task, although no stress should be placed upon their putting the sentences back together "correctly." The fun comes in getting them combined in incorrect but amusing ways.

As a check on their knowledge of and skill in language conventions, you can ask your students these questions at the end of the first part of the activity:

- How did you know where the sentences started?

- What do you call those groups of words that start with "who"?

- What do you call the group of words that have a verb in them?

- What do you call a group of words that begins with "from" or "with"?

After your students have played around with putting together some bizarre sentences, they are invited to draw a cartoon with a "wacky" sentence of their choice as its caption. This will provide an opportunity for them to get away from words and use other talents.

Following Through

Depending upon the success of the activity, you could make a display of the cartoons produced. Excellent efforts can be featured in a class or school periodical.

GRANDMOTHERS AND TRAFFIC COPS

1. The following groups of words were originally eight separate sentences. These fairly sensible statements were each broken up into three parts and then mixed up as you see them below. See if you can put them together again as they were originally intended to be.

who hate business	often annoy teachers	Businessmen
Traffic cops	Mountain climbers	may cause accidents
make good baby sitters	with poor vision	Housewives
Football players	are happiest when playing	are familiar with pain
who dance in the kitchen	seldom become wealthy	Musicians
are uncomfortable in small cars	who chew gum	who refuse to wear shoes
who are hard-of-hearing	Grandmothers are considered odd by	Children
who love their work	their neighbors	who weigh more than three hundred pounds

a. _____

_____

b. _____

_____

c. _____

_____

d. _____

_____

e. _____

_____

f. _____

_____

g. _____

_____

h. _____

_____

2. Did you come up with some rather unusual ideas when you were trying to piece together the eight sentences? Just for fun, write down the craziest sentences that you came up with in the space below, along with other ridiculous sentences that you can make out of the groups of words given above.

_____

_____

_____

_____

_____

_____

Which is your favorite sentence? Why is it your favorite sentence?

3. Take your favorite "wacky" sentence and do something with it. Draw a cartoon and use your sentence as a captionin the space below.

Activity Beanbag Game (10-20 minutes)
Material beanbag

Arrange your students in a circle. Explain that when one player has the beanbag he is to say a word just as he tosses it to any other player. The player catching the beanbag is to give just two words or items that go with the word that was spoken and then sum them up. (This should be done quickly.) That player in turn says a word and tosses the beanbag to another player, and the procedure is repeated until your students run out of ideas. Typical prompts and responses:

Prompt	Response
now	and then – occasionally
snap	crackle, pop – cereal
Los Angeles	San Francisco, Eureka – Highway 101
Tom	Dick, Harry – ordinary guys
Hart	Schaffner, Marx – suits
red	white, blue – American flag
double	your pleasure – gum
more	or less – approximately
Wizard	of Oz – book (movie)
Yellow	brick road – Wizard of Oz
over	the rainbow – Judy Garland
on	a roll – winning streak
forward	guard, center – basketball
3	5, 7 – arithmetic progression
5	10, 20 – 35
fine	and dandy – good
never	say die – determination

References Parnes, S. J. (1975). Aha! Insights into Creative Behavior. East Aurora, N.Y.: D.O.K. Publishers.

"SEEING WITH IMAGINATION"

The theme of this lesson is **visualization**. Your students are invited to make images that go hand in hand with creative thinking. They are also invited to reflect about imagery in language.

Thinking skills emphasized

- **visualizing richly and colorfully**
- being original
- letting humor flow
- looking at it in a different way
- analyzing
- making judgments

Some educational psychologists (Dacey, 1976; Khatena, 1984) believe that the right hemisphere style of learning is becoming more prominent because today's elementary, high school, and college students have experienced television for their entire lives. The ability to visualize events, concepts, systems, and processes of all kinds is considered by many authorities to be the sine qua non for advances in scientific, artistic, philosophical, and athletic endeavors.

Khatena (1984) maintains that imagery, in its fluid and least culture-determined state, can be regarded as "the language of discovery."

Activity Sketching the Misconceptions of Children When Trying to Grasp Metaphors (45-50 minutes)
Writing a Converstation Containing Two Metaphors
(30-45 minutes)
Activity Sheet "Flying Females"

Introducing the Activity

If your students have younger siblings, they are well aware of how literally young children can take language. Since our language is laced so heavily with figures of speech, life can be confusing to the very young and often to those older. If you have a favorite story about a child taking an expression literally, that anecdote would be an ideal way to introduce this unit. We use a couple of metaphors that can cause children problems, but you may well have a better example. And your pupils probably have some good ones, too.

Administering the Activity

Most of the misconceptions that children have when they take language too literally are humorous, and so this activity attempts to capitalize upon that element by conjuring up images of women flying off handles and into "rages." We ask your students to sketch their ideas of these misconceptions instead of explaining them in words. One reason for not asking for a written description is that it is natural to get a picture of the misguided notion. We also think it is a good idea to encourage those pupils who are good at representing their ideas graphically to do so occasionally.

Because it is so common for children to misinterpret metaphorical expressions and because they are not so far removed from the days when they were doing the misinterpreting, your students should readily identify with the confusion wrought by metaphors among young children. A natural lead-in to the unit would be to ask for examples of children who became confused by adults using various figures of speech. You should be able to get a number of good examples.

At the second level of involvement reintroduce your pupils to the term metaphor. What do you imagine when you hear "That's a whale of a problem"? Ask them to recall some occasions when people have used them in their speech. When one becomes conscious of figures of speech such as the metaphor, it is really surprising how often they are used.

You'll want to make sure that your pupils can differentiate between a metaphor and a simile before they listen for metaphors in the speech of others. It would seem to be appropriate, then, to check them out on the differences. By giving a few of each kind to the class, you will be able to see if they are really able to identify metaphors. Give them expressions orally. Here are a few that could be used:

He pulled that off as slick as a whistle. (Simile)
The line hit the ball carrier like a ton of bricks. (Simile)
The crowd spilled over on to the field of play. (Metaphor)
He steamed into the office and shouted at the man behind the desk. (Metaphor)
After her boss criticized her, Penny went into her shell. (metaphor)

After listening for metaphors in the conversations of friends and others, it shouldn't be very difficult to compose a conversation that has two metaphors. As a matter of fact, if your students are able to, they might reproduce conversations that they actually have heard.

If lessons in writing direct quotations have been taught recently, a brief review of the different kinds of quotations and their punctuation might be done before your pupils begin the third part of the unit. For some, a review of the difference between quoting directly and quoting indirectly would also be in order. Your students will learn once again the importance of knowing how to use punctuation marks accurately while they are engaged in this activity.

Following Through

In subsequent writing assignments you will have many opportunities to observe whether your students have made use of metaphors. If they are advanced in expressing themselves, the frequency with which they use metaphors may not pick up. On the other hand, becoming more aware of this figure of speech may increase its use by those students who were relatively unaccustomed to enlivening their writing with metaphorical language.

Allow 15-20 minutes in class for any of the following three activities, or assign one of them or the fourth activity as homework.

• Have your students pair off. One student describes something such as a cat, house, dress, toy, car, et al. and the other student sketches it. Then they reverse roles.

• Give your students each 20-24 colored bits of paper. They can be squares or triangles, and there should be at least four colors represented (for example, 5 of white, 5 of gold, 5 of red, and 5 of purple). Challenge them to make something lovely or striking by combining the bits of paper.

• Play some modern classical music on the CD player, preferably by one of the composers who uses an electronic/synthesizer technique. Ask your students to sketch any scene that the music suggests to them.

• In the next 24 hours your students are to look at whatever they ordinarily look at, but they are to look as if what they see they are seeing for the first time. They are to record everything that had gone unnoticed previously.

Reference

Myers, R.E. (2002) Word Play: Language Lessons for Creative Learners. Marion IL: Pieces of Learning.

FLYING FEMALES

A. Young children sometimes take what we say quite literally – and it confuses them. They are confused by how we express ourselves sometimes, as when we use expressions such as "June flew off the handle yesterday when her husband told her he'd lost his paycheck." Upon hearing that sentence, a child might see a woman clutching a big handle and then flying away from it. When children hear expressions such as "She flew into a rage" and "Harry went into a tizzy," visions of a woman flying like Peter Pan into something called a "rage" or a young man walking into a place called a "tizzy" may come into their minds.

Imagine what a confused child would visualize when he or she hears the following expressions. Draw a sketch of each of the scenes that might come to the child's mind.

Terry let Bob down by not showing up for work again.	She tore into him after the guests left.
Jim was all puffed up because he had won the prize.	He made a donkey of himself at the party last night.

B. It's not hard to hear expressions such as those we've given; you hear them all the time. You can probably hear dozens if you listen carefully during the next 24 hours. Try to remember at least four and write them down in the space below. This kind of expression is called a <u>metaphor</u>. It occurs when words that are generally used in one field of experience are used in another, such as in the expression, "Don't make a pig of yourself." You understand what "making a pig of yourself" means, but if you took the saying literally it would be telling you not to change yourself into an animal (if you did have the magic power to do so).

SOME METAPHORS I'VE HEARD

1. _____

2. _____

3. _____

4. _____

C. During the past 24 hours you've probably heard a few of the most common metaphors in our language, and you just may have heard one or two that were unusual. Some expressions are found only in a particular part of the country, and they sound strange when a native of that region says them outside his or her area. Write a conversation between two people that has at least two metaphors in it. The conversation can be one you heard or one you can imagine being spoken.

_____

_____

_____

_____

_____

_____

_____

_____

Extension

Activity Recording Colorful Expressions (homework, ongoing)
Materials pencil, notebook, notepad or sheet of paper
Activity Sheet "Catching Color"

To reinforce their feeling for color in language, you might assign your students the task of listening for colorful or effective language. You could say: **I believe you are getting a better appreciation of the variety and color we have in the English language. I want you to listen to how people express themselves, and then write the best examples of colorful speech. This is just something that you can do casually. You can make a list.**

Notes

CATCHING COLOR

Record the expressions you hear or read that you believe to be particularly colorful or effective. Your sources for an informal survey of picturesque language are almost limitless. You can "monitor" the speech of your classmates, of salespeople, of television and movie personalities, or people in public places, newspaper reporters, magazine writers, novelists, poets, laborers, your parents and other relatives.

You might want to keep adding to your list for several weeks. Maybe you will be surprised to learn where the best sources of colorful expressions turn out to be.

Activity Making up Colorful Definitions for Well-Known Things
(25-30 minutes)
Activity Sheet "Definitions"
Materials pencil, pen, crayons, felt pens, colored chalk

Introducing the Activity

This activity is a lighthearted one. In introducing "Definitions" you might say a few words about colorful language. You can assure your students that they won't be subjected to a quiz – in fact, no dictionary would help them very much. They'll mostly have to use their imaginations.

Administering the Activity

At the first level of involvement, five fanciful definitions are given for your students to translate, and then the process is reversed with 10 definitions to invent for words such as bumblebee and necktie at the second level. The second task is the more difficult one, although both are challenging. Other items that could possibly inspire colorful definitions and that might be added to those in the activity are: a clock, a bear, an airplane, a hot dog, an accordion, and a turtle.

Following Through

After "Definitions" this activity might follow:

Say: **Imagine that you heard a crash and then heard a cough and then felt a gust of cold air. What would you think it was? Draw a picture of it in pencil. Then add some color and give it a label.**

If you have time, you could add this one:

Imagine that you smelled something burning and then heard water running and then heard a laugh. What would you think it was? Draw a picture of the scene. Then add some color and label it.

DEFINITIONS

Do you know what a definition is? Where can you go when you want to find out what a strange word means?

Sometimes people come up with their own words for things. For example, a "dayshiner" might be a one-word definition for the sun. You could call a porcupine a "moving pincushion" or a camel a "walking hill." People used to call doctors "sawbones" and dogs "fleabags."

What are these brief definitions describing?

1. a black-and-white smellevision _____

2. a giant banana in orbit _____

3. a flittery, fluttery flyer _____

4. a spotted derrick _____

5. a feathered alarm clock _____

Come up with your own definitions of these words.

1. A bumblebee is _____

2. A necktie is _____

3. A zebra is _____

4. A street is _____

5. An airplane is _____

6. A cloud is _____

7. Suspenders are _____

8. A telephone is _____

9. A raccoon is _____

10. A parrot is _____

LESSON 12

"FANTASTIC"

The most enduring elements in any culture are its myths and fairy tales. They are passed along from generation to generation endlessly. Although they can be changed in detail, they remain essentially the same because of the truths they tell about the people. We hold myths and fairy tales dear throughout life; it's only the subjects – the heroes and villains – that change names as we grow older.

Thinking skills emphasized

- **enjoying and using fantasy**
- being original
- combining and synthesizing
- producing alternatives
- letting humor flow
- analyzing

Russell (1956) felt that fantasies in young people are not unhealthy but should be kept alive until their intellectual development is such that they can engage in more realistic types of thinking. He believed that fantasies such as **imaginative role playing, telling fantastic stories, and drawing** in fanciful or even weird ways should be considered normal.

Activity Writing a Purposely False Account of a Situation or Development (25 minutes)
Activity Sheet "The Facts Are Irrelevant"

Introducing the Activity

This activity can provide a change of pace for writing assignments. It makes fibbing legitimate and should thereby prove liberating to your students. To assure your students that it is all right to lie, you might say: **Take the directions in this activity literally – you can fib all you want . . . but you only have 20 minutes to do it.**

The time limitation will also be liberating because your students won't have time to worry too much about the formal aspects of their writing. They can do it in a kind of stream of consciousness mode.

Administering the Activity

You don't have to be told that your main problem in administering this activity is to keep your students from getting too silly. One way of keeping the lid on is to have an attitude that the prevarication is rather serious and the activity itself is nothing too unusual. It's unlikely that your being serious about the activity will dampen your students' enthusiasm for a chance to lie.

Following Through

A variety of activities can follow the completion of the fantastic stories, but first you must decide whether to have your students revise and correct their stories or to just let the activity stand as a diversion. Among the activities that could follow "The Facts Are Irrelevant" are these:

- Have your students illustrate their stories.

- Have them create headlines that could be published if the stories were real.

- Select one of the stories and have the class as a whole write a sequel to it.

- Present all of the stories on a bulletin board or in a booklet (but they must be in readable form).

- If a story is appropriate for a student publication, the writer could revise and polish it.

Notes

THE FACTS ARE IRRELEVANT

Isn't it more fun to ignore the facts sometimes? It can be a lot more fun. We can just say and write things that please us or justify our actions or fit our prejudices. Why bother sticking to the facts? It's not so much fun as disregarding them.

Ignoring whatever facts you may be aware of, choose one of the following and write as much as you can in about 20 minutes.

- Describe your next shopping trip.

- Tell about the vehicle you will be buying.

- Predict how your team will do next year.

- Tell what your chances are for accumulating wealth.

- Describe your next vacation.

- Predict the results of your next test.

- Tell how you'll overcome the obstacle that has hindered you most of the past year.

Extensions

Activity Writing a Tall Tale (50 minutes)
Activity Sheet "Now I'll Tell One"

The tall tale is a sub-species of the fairy tale, and that is the genre that your students are to engage in with this activity. As the title indicates, they are to assume the role of the great exaggerators, such as Baron Munchausen, in spinning their tall tales. You can lead in to the activity by saying:

We may not admit it, but most of us like to stretch the truth a little to make a better story. Here is a chance for you to let that tendency take hold of you – you can exaggerate to your heart's content in writing a tall tale. Tall tales have always been popular in every part of the world, and so you'll be following a universal and time-honored tradition.

Notes

NOW I'LL TELL ONE

Here are three stories.

* Paul Bunyan once had a very unusual farm. Everything on it seemed to grow terribly large. Indeed, the size of things embarrassed Paul. The chickens laid extremely large eggs. When a chicken wanted to lay an egg, she had to get five other chickens to help her. Paul's corn grew very rapidly. When it started growing, it never stopped. Therefore, it became extremely tall. Paul could not chop down this corn. It grew so fast his ax never struck the same place twice. One day, a little boy laboriously climbed up one of the corn stalks. After a week of climbing, he finally reached the top. Then he tried to come down. The stalk, however, was growing faster than the boy could slide down. He is probably still up there.

* Marvin is an avid circus fan. When the circus comes to town, he goes every day. This year he was especially impressed with the fat lady, "Big Bertha." He kept wondering how she moved around and who made her clothes for her. One day he gathered enough courage to ask her a few questions. He was told she was staying at a hotel nearby. When Marvin knocked on the door of her room, a slim woman opened the door.

"I'd like to see Big Bertha, please," Marvin said.
"I'm Big Bertha," the woman responded.
"Oh, I mean the lady who works in the circus," he said.
"That's me. I work in the circus, but this is my day off."

* Matilda Tippets wanted to be a famous singer. From the time she was a little girl she imagined herself singing to people in theaters and auditoriums all over the world. She just knew that she would become a marvelous singer. Since her parents wanted to be kind, they didn't tell Matilda that she had one of the worst singing voices they had ever heard. It turned out that Matilda was tone deaf.

As she grew older, Matilda began to sing more often. She sang as she came to breakfast, and the milk curdled. She sang before she brushed her teeth, and the bristles fell out of her toothbrush. She sang to her dolls, she sang to her mirror, and she sang to her dog. The dog always howled and ran away when she did that. One day, Matilda heard the birds singing outside. She ran out and tried to sing with them. Two birds fell from the trees, never to twitter and fly again.

Finally, after an eventful girlhood, Matilda met someone who didn't want to leave suddenly when she began to sing. In a short time they were engaged. Later, when they were married, she sang everyday in the kitchen. Although they had to buy a lot of milk, they were happy. Her husband admired Matilda a lot. Of course, he was tone deaf, too.

What kind of tall tale do you like best – ones that are funny or full of marvelous happenings, or those that are outrageous?

When you write a tall tale, you can keep these points in mind:

1. The teller of a tall tale doesn't expect to be believed.

2. A tall tale can be used on an actual event, or series of events, that is elaborated upon and exaggerated.

3. Tall tales always contain exaggerations; they can be fantastic, preposterous and/or grotesque.

4. Like a good short story, a tall tale should end with something of a surprise.

Write a short tall tale!

_____

_____

_____

_____

_____

_____

_____

_____

_____

_____

_____

_____

_____

Activity Writing "New" Fairy Tales (45-50 minutes)
Activity Sheet "Fairy Tales Revisited"

If your students are in the middle grades they may think it beneath them to write a fairy tale. This activity won't offend them, however, because it has them mixing up the familiar plots in a whimsical way. For instance, the first suggestion for a "new" fairy tale is "The Ugly New Clothes," a combination of "The Ugly Duckling" and "The Emperor's New Clothes." Of course, the new fairy tale doesn't have to resemble either of those two stories.

Introducing the Activity

It might be a good idea to read a fairy tale to your students before giving them "Fairy Tales Revisited." Many fairy tales are brief, and you can quickly set the mood for this activity. Among Andersen's stories, "The Princess and the Pea" is quite short and would be suitable. Of the Grimm's fairy tales, "The Three Lazy Bones" is very short and has a good surprise ending. Another of the Grimm's tales, "The Queen Bee," is also brief, and it is a good example of the "Cinderella"-"Snow White" type of fairy tale.

Administering the Activity

Only six titles of mixed-up fairy tales are listed in the activity, but you may want to add a few to give your students more combinations. For example, "The Princess and the Queen Bee" or "The Queen Bee and the Princess" would be appropriate if you read those two tales. You also might encourage your students to propose other combinations.

Following Through

The logical outcome of this activity is to have your students read aloud their compositions. If you want to review their productions first to ensure that they are not too silly or in bad taste, you might monitor their work as they are writing or have the tales turned in to you. (It is probably wise not to stress the mechanical and formal elements of this writing activity, or the fun will be taken out of it.) Because this kind of writing is enhanced by illustration, some students might want to collaborate with others in producing something that can be displayed or placed in a collection of fairy tales by the class.

FAIRY TALES REVISITED

If we mix up the titles of fairy tales and come up with new titles, we can get some good ideas for new tales. For example, if we mix up "The Emperor's New Clothes" with "Puss in Boots," the new title could be "The Emperor's New Boots," and that might suggest a story about what happened when an emperor purchased new boots. The boots might have been too tight, they might have annoyed the empress because they squeaked, or they might have been made of a magic material. There are any number of plots that can be produced to go with that title.

Come up with just one plot for these "new" fairy tales. You can choose from one of these six titles, or you can combine the titles of a couple of other fairy tales.

The Ugly New Clothes   Jack and the Three Bears

The Gingerbread Boots   Snow White and the Three Bears

The Three Little Musicians   Sleeping Beauty and the Three
                                    Little Pigs

What is your new fairy tale called? Use the space below to write your story.

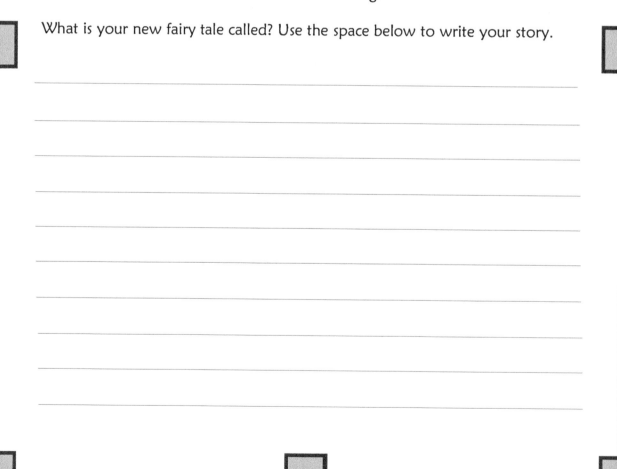

Activity Collective Storytelling (30-45 minutes)

Circular Lying

Alternately, instead of administering a writing activity, you can give your students some practice in listening, using the same theme of untruth-telling. Have your students form a large circle. Tell them that the main idea of the activity is to tell a story collectively in which everything said is totally untrue. The story should have a fair amount of action, and the characters should express a wide range of emotions. Other than these three requirements, no other constraints upon the storytelling are necessary. The listening skills of your students will be brought sharply into play because each student must listen carefully to the speaker as the story progresses.

Reference

Russell, D. (1956). <u>Children's Thinking</u>. Boston: Ginn.

Notes

"SWINGING"

More and more educators are becoming convinced that it is all right for young people to learn with more than just their eyes and ears. They now believe that **learning from bodily movement, music, and rhythm** is permissible in the classroom. We've known for many years that some young people prefer to learn from movement, music, and rhythm and that all students can profit from using more than one sense modality at a time.

Thinking skills emphasized

- **making it swing, making it ring**
- being original
- orienting to the future
- analyzing
- making judgments
- hypothesizing

Torrance (1999) cautions that the **kinesthetically** gifted student may not respond to a purely verbal teaching style. Studies of the various styles of learning with regard to the brain's two hemispheres seem to confirm what many educators have observed as to the differing preferences children have for learning.

Responsiveness to the kinesthetic includes "not only manipulative movements but also kinesthetic discrimination, psychomotor coordination, endurance, strength, flexibility, adaptive motor skills, expressive movement, and interpretive movement" (Torrance, 1999, p. 189). Common examples of auditory responsiveness include that the individual writes, draws, walks, and moves in rhythm; creates songs; is facilitated in learning of skills and understanding of ideas by rhythm; interprets ideas, events, and feelings through rhythm and music; and works perseveringly at music and rhythmic activities. Two of Gardner's (1993) multiple intelligences – rhythmic-musical and bodily-kinesthetic – also give support for the use of these skills in school.

Activity Demonstrating Learning Through Movement (25-35 minutes)
Activity Sheet "Learning by Moving"

Introducing the Activity

You can lead into this activity with a few gestures that signify disgust (holding your nose), uncertainty (shrugging your shoulders), shaky feelings (tipping your hand from side to side), respect (bowing), dejection (drooping your shoulders or hanging your head), exasperation (kicking your foot out). Your students can readily understand the meaning of each bodily gesture, and so they will be warmed up for the activity.

Then say: **To do this exercise, you won't have to do very much writing. You'll be asked to do some moving around. Then you can report what you have experienced.**

Pass out "Learning by Moving" so that they can get an idea of what they are to do.

Administering the Activity

The activity is meant to be engaged in by the entire class. You should tell your students to look it over but that they won't be doing any writing just yet. Ask for volunteers for each gesture only after everyone has had time to think about the task. After a student responds, ask if there are other ways to do the task. There may be several interpretations. When they write their experiences, tell your students to be reflective about what they learned from performing the tasks.

Following Through

One of the best ways to follow up "Learning by Moving" is to have your students engage in a creative dramatics session. You might select any of the following themes:

• "Is It a Dream?" You wake up one morning and look out the window to see if the sun is shining. It is. In fact, the sunlight is blinding. But when you look at the front yard, you see a giraffe looking for something to eat . . .

• "It's Bitterly Cold." Climbing one of the highest mountains in the world, we are blasted by a bitterly cold wind. We look for some shelter, but when we try to crawl under a ledge we find something that scares us witless . . .

• "On an Unknown Planet." We're forced to land on an unknown planet because of a malfunction of our instruments. When we look through the windows of our space craft, we see rocks that seem to be bouncing around on the ground and lots of shimmering, glittering bits of things in the air . . .

• "Inside a Giant Coconut." We're walking in a wild, weird jungle when we encounter what looks like a huge ball. It's a coconut! Amazingly, a door opens in the side of the coconut and we enter it . . .

LEARNING BY MOVING

You use your body in all kinds of ways. But did you know that your body also helps you to learn? Let's see how this works. Follow the directions for doing some of the usual tasks you do in school. Later on, you can think about what happened and write it down.

Spelling and Handwriting

1. Show the way your name looks without using paper or pencil.

2. Only with your hands, show the difference between "two" and "to." Then demonstrate the difference in pantomime.

3. With your hands, show how "receive" should be spelled.

Punctuation

1. Demonstrate with your body the difference between a semi-colon and a period.

2. Describe the <u>look</u> of a question mark with movement from your body.

3. Describe the <u>meaning</u> of a question mark with movement from your body.

4. Describe the <u>look</u> of an exclamation mark with movement from your body.

5. Describe the <u>meaning</u> of an exclamation mark with movement from your body.

Grammar

1. Demonstrate, without words, the difference between an active verb and a passive verb.

2. Demonstrate, without words, the difference between the nominative and objective forms of a pronoun (such as "I" and "me").

What Were Your Experiences?

<u>Spelling and Handwriting</u>

Did moving your hands help you remember the difference between "two" and "to"? If so, how?

_____

_____

Did moving your hands help you to remember how to spell "receive"? If so, how?

_____

_____

Punctuation

Did your experiences in showing the difference between a semi-colon and a period help you remember the difference? If so, how?

_____

_____

Did your experiences in describing the look and meaning of a question mark reinforce your understanding of that punctuation mark? If so, how?

_____

_____

Did describing the look and meaning of an exclamation mark reinforce your understanding of its use? If so, how?

_____

_____

Grammar

Did demonstrating, without words, the difference between an active and a passive verb increase your understanding of the differences? If so, how?

_____

_____

Did demonstrating, without words, the difference between the nominative and objective forms of a pronoun help you remember the differences? If so, how?

_____

_____

Extensions

Activity Imagining Eleven Sounds and Identifying Sounds That Make You
Feel Good, Uneasy, and Alert (initial session 25-30 minutes)
Materials cowbell or dinner bell, balloon, comb, tissue paper,
water glass, straw
Activity Sheet "Using Your Ears"

For a great many years Torrance has been calling attention to the roles that auditory and
kinesthetic modalities play in creative performance. Recently this theme has been picked up by
Gardner (1982, 1993), Armstrong (1993), and others in the Multiple Intelligences movement.
Torrance noted: "Children, if not inhibited by societal restraint, seem to use their kinesthetic and
auditory senses naturally to facilitate their creative function" (1999, p. 187). He goes on to say
that "if the thinker can experience something kinesthetically and auditorily it gives him or her a
firmer grasp of the information, and this increases the chances of a larger number of useful, valid
alternatives . . . Just experiencing something through two or more sense modalities seems to
help a person attain exciting insights that he or she would otherwise miss" (1999, pp. 187-88).

Although there have been attempts to give listening a more prominent place in the
language arts curriculum, teachers have generally given much less attention to listening skills
than they have to spelling or handwriting. The truth is, listening is fun for the teacher and fun
for the student. We sincerely hope that you are not ignoring it.

Introducing the Activity

To get your students in the proper mood for this activity, you might play a little game
with them. Have a student accomplice go into an adjoining room or behind a screen, if there is
one available. If you use an adjoining room, leave the door ajar. Instruct him to make four
sounds, in this order:

1. Ring a cowbell or a dinner bell.

2. Slurp the last of a glass of water with a straw.

3. Blow up a balloon and let the air escape (not letting go of the balloon).

4. Finally, put some tissue paper over a comb and blow on it.

Ask the students to refrain from saying anything until after your accomplice makes the
fourth sound. Then they can identify the four sounds in their correct order. Allow about 10
minutes for this part of the activity.

Administering the Activity

This activity is concerned with using the sense of hearing, that is, encouraging your students to be more alert and discerning listeners. It takes time for students to respond to all of the questions and suggestions that are put to them, and so the all-important time factor should be kept in mind. You can't administer this activity in an ordinary class period. Two sessions are suggested, but it might take a week for some students to complete it.

Your students are asked to imagine 11 events and sensations in order to get them in the mood to use their ears efficiently. Next, there are questions about how sounds make them feel. Then your students are to locate 11 sounds, all of which can be found in their everyday lives (a sound that stops people, one that puts people to sleep, and so forth). Finally, they are asked to imagine where 11 sounds could be found 20 years from now. Will sounds play as big a role in their lives in two decades, or will there be changes that make the sense of hearing even more important?

Following Through

This activity can follow "Using Your Ears." Allow 15-20 minutes for it, but the length of time will depend upon how well your students listen and how involved they become in the activity. Read the following:

PANTOMIME

In this activity students will be asked to do no talking. They are to express themselves in the movements of their bodies. First, have them think a little bit about how people move, how they use their hands, and how they carry themselves.

Here are three stereotypical individuals. Read the description of the first and then be prepared to interpret that individual's personality in pantomime.

Individual #1:

This man is young, but he's not quite as young as he'd like to be. He was a fairly good athlete in high school, having played football and thrown the shot in track. Most of his exercise since high school has come from driving a truck, walking from the dinner table to the television set, and getting on and off bar stools. He is married, but his wife and one child see less of him than his buddies do.

Select a short series of movements to portray the personality of Individual #1 at the front of the classroom.

Here is a second type of person you may be familiar with – or even think you know. Read the description and then think of the characteristic moves and mannerisms that highlight her personality.

Individual #2:

She has been called frivolous and an "air-head." But she doesn't mind. What she cares most about is being noticed and being among a group of her friends. She isn't dull-witted; in fact, she makes better grades than most people would think. Quite a few people admire her because she's pretty and dresses smartly.

After thinking of how this young person uses her hands, holds her head, uses facial expressions, and moves around in a group, select a few of these movements and expressions to illustrate her personality.

For the third individual, try an entirely different type of person. After reading a little about him, close your eyes and try to visualize how he looks and how he acts.

Individual #3:

He is as self-conscious as Individual #2, but in a different way. In his middle-age years, this person is shy, meticulous, and dignified. He suffers from aslight inferiority complex that is intensified somewhat because he has been a bank teller for 20 years. This gentleman wears eyeglasses and conservative suits. You've seen him.

Pick out a few characteristic movements that depict this individual's personality and put them together in front of the class.

Notes

132

USING YOUR EARS

1. How sharp are your senses? An important part of using your brain is using all of your senses. Most people don't. Imagine the things below that stir up your senses. Try to imagine:

the sensation of falling

the crunch of crackers

the taste of orange juice

the smell of vinegar

the feel of velvet

the sound of a car's tires skidding

the sound of crickets at night

the feel of mud between your toes

the sound of someone sneezing

the sound of the pages of a newspaper being turned

the smell of burnt rubber

2. Are there sounds that almost always make you feel good? What are they?

_____

_____

_____

How can you use those sounds in order to be happier and more productive?

_____

_____

_____

_____

3. Are there sounds that almost always make you uneasy? What are they?

_____

How can you use those sounds to your advantage?

_____

_____

_____

4. Are there sounds that usually make you more alert? What are they?

_____

_____

_____

Are you using them to help you? If so, how are you using them?

_____

_____

_____

If not, how could you be using those sounds to help you?

_____

_____

_____

5. Just from thinking about sounds that made you feel good or uneasy and those that made you run, you can see how important sounds are. We can't escape from them unless we are totally deaf. Do some more thinking about sounds. In the next 24 hours search for some sounds. You probably won't have to go far to find most of them, but you will have to keep your ears open. None of these sounds is impossible to find, but you may not be able to determine the exact location of a few. If you can't actually hear the sounds, tell where you would be in order to hear them. But before you do your sound detective work, think about what sound is. Exactly what is sound? Now look in the dictionary and find the definition of the noun sound. What does your dictionary say sound is?

Now that you have a good idea of what sound can be, do some sound sleuthing.

a. Find a sound that calls dogs. Describe it.

   Where did you find it?

b. Find a sound that stops people. Describe it.

   Where did you find it?

c. Find a sound that wakes people. Describe it.

   Where did you find it?

d. Find a sound that puts people to sleep. Describe it.

   Where did you find it?

e. Find a sound that warns people. Describe it.

   Where did you find it?

f. Find a sound that hurts people. Describe it.

   Where did you find it?

g. Find a sound that closes minds. Describe it.

   Where did you find it?

h. Find a sound that opens minds. Describe it.

   Where did you find it?

i. Find a sound that opens doors. Describe it.

   Where did you find it?

j. Find a sound that opens hearts. Describe it.

   Where did you find it?

k. Find a sound that makes money. Describe it.

   Where did you find it?

6. Where would you expect to find these sounds about 20 years from now?

A sound that:

a. rewards _____

b. punishes _____

c. makes plants grow _____

d. deceives _____

e. helps people lose weight _____

f. makes people angry _____

g. makes people relaxed or sleepy _____

h. makes people energetic _____

i. makes people forgetful _____

j. makes animals grow _____

k. paralyzes _____

Activity Demonstrating Learning Through Rhythm

RHYTHMIC LEARNING

You can give your students practice in **rhythmic sensitivity** by having them do the following. Say to them:

• By using only your hands, demonstrate the walk of a lame man with a cane.

• Without using real words – only sounds similar to words – show how a limerick goes.

• By using only your hands, show how a rap song goes.

• Use either your mouth or your hands to show the difference between the first 15 minutes of school and the last 15 minutes.

• Demonstrate the difference between the rhythm of unlocking a door and starting up a car.

• By using your mouth and hands, show how a pitcher pitches to a catcher. (Make believe you are doing the sound effects for a radio program.)

Allow about 20-25 minutes for the activity.

References

Armstrong, T. (1993). Seven Kinds of Smart: Identifying and Developing Many Kinds of Intelligence. Tucson, AZ: Zephyr Press.

Gardner, H. (1982). Frames of the Mind. New York: Basic Books.

Gardner, H. (1993). Multiple Intelligences: The Theory in Practice. New York: Basic Books.

Torrance, E. P. and H. T. Safter (1999). Making the Creative Leap Beyond. Buffalo, N.Y.: Creative Education Foundation Press.

"ANOTHER WAY"

This lesson encourages your students to see different perspectives of things and also to appreciate the individual who sees life differently from others.

Thinking skills emphasized

- **looking at it in another way**
- letting humor flow
- being original
- visualizing richly and colorfully
- analyzing

The main creative thinking skill called for in this lesson is **looking at it in another way**. Torrance (Torrance and Safter, 1999) had conception as well as perception in mind in designating this as an important creative thinking skill. How we look at ourselves and the world around us is crucial to maintaining a safe and healthy existence; but when we produce novel ideas, we must experience sensations in a fresh, spontaneous way.

In every area of creative endeavor the individuals who can perceive things differently are the ones who make significant contributions in their fields. If a young person consistently perceives phenomena and situations differently from her peers, she may be genuinely creative – someone who needs to be encouraged because she does see things differently and may be viewed as odd.

Activity Perceiving Apparently Negative Events in a Positive Way (30-45 minutes)
Activity Sheet "Looking At It In Another Way"

Introducing the Activity

You might introduce the activity by citing an experience you had that seemed horrible at the time but which turned out much better than you anticipated, such as performing very badly (as in cooking or dancing) and then being determined to do it very well – and becoming expert at it.

Administering the Activity

Some events may seem very unfortunate or even disastrous, but they can also be seen as having positive aspects. For instance, a forest fire can kill plants and animals, but it can also help them by removing undergrowth and allowing more light to reach the trees. A forest fire can enrich the soil with nitrogen and potash, thus providing better grass upon which many animals will graze.

Your students can probably come up with a wide variety of responses to the seven questions, and these might be among them:

1. Stumbling might forcibly bring the person's attention to her faulty vision. An eye examination may be called for.

2. Coming down with the measles might mean catching up on your reading or getting around to doing a project you have wanted to do.

3. Receiving an unwanted gift can help you to learn to be gracious.

4. Spilling my milk helped make my mother more patient. I'm not sure if she were grateful for it, though.

5. The derailment of a train might mean extra wages for the workers who put the train back on the track.

6. Being broke is seldom a blessing, but it might keep a person from making an unwise purchase or give her a legitimate excuse to turn down a chronic borrower.

7. Failing a test has been a "wake-up call" for many students who could do much better, and then did.

Following Through

To reinforce the skill of seeing things from a different perspective you might ask your students to look at things from the viewpoint of a dog or a cat. For instance, you might ask them if they were a cat or a dog, how would they interpret these events:

1. A fish (covered in paper) somehow slips out of a grocery van when it is making a delivery to a home.

How will the cat view the event?

How will the dog view the event?

How will the owner of the grocery view the event?

2. A two-year-old boy is playing with a balloon in a park. A gust of wind blows the balloon from his hands, and it skips over a bush.

How will a cat view the event?

How will a dog view the event?

How will the boy view the event?

3. A boy's best friend comes into his house to listen to music. Suddenly he grabs the boy's hat and they wrestle.

How will the dog view the event?

How will the cat view the event?

How will the boy's mother view the event?

Notes

LOOKING AT IT IN ANOTHER WAY

1. What good can come of a person stumbling repeatedly when walking on a rough path?

2. How can coming down with the measles help anyone?

3. How could receiving a gift you never will use be a good thing for you?

4. How could spilling milk at the dinner table benefit anyone?

5. In what way could a train's getting derailed help someone?

6. How could being broke be a blessing in disguise?

7. How might failing a test work to someone's advantage?

Extensions

Activity Using Baseball to Teach Courses in School (20-30 minutes)
Materials baseball or softball, glove, wooden bat

Display a baseball (softball), glove, and bat before the class. After they are seen by all of your students, say: **What have I got here? Yes, a ball, a bat, and a glove. These could be valuable teaching tools. Do you know how? Well, I'm not going to tell you. Can you tell me how I could use each of these things to teach here at school?**

Let them ponder the question, and then use these prompts:

• How could I use one of these items to help me to teach <u>Math</u>? (baseball: calculating speed in flight, diameter, circumference, measuring resilience or bounce, and the like; glove: measuring linear dimensions, weight, diameter of the pocket, and the like; bat: measuring dimensions, weight, circumference of the barrel and handle, and so forth)

• How could I use one of them to help me teach <u>science</u>? (baseball: density, gravity, determine whether or not it is covered with cowhide, discuss advantages and disadvantages of coverings, laws of motion; bat: determine species and characteristics of wood; glove: determine type and origin of leather, discuss advantages and disadvantages of various kinds of leather or other materials)

• How could I use one of these items to help me teach <u>geography</u>? (baseball, glove, and bat: place of manufacture, cities in the state that use the type of ball, bat and glove and others either involved in distribution or sale of the three)

• How could I use one of these items to teach <u>art</u>? (baseball: subject of a still life drawing, cartoon figure of a person in the shape of the ball; bat: cartoon figure of a person in the shape of a bat: glove: subject of a still life drawing; arrangement of all three objects in an esthetically pleasing way)

• How could I use one of these items to teach <u>language arts</u>? (baseball, bat, and glove: writing an imaginary conversation among the three; autobiography, factual account of manufacture and/or distribution)

If any of these suggestions or others coming from the class prove to be stimulating – for instance, if the idea of an autobiography appeals to your students – you might have them engage in the activity. Time is the limiting factor, of course.

Activity Discussing the Ramifications of Reversing Our Society's Expectations
(30 minutes)

This "What Would Happen If" activity is probably better administered as a discussion. Say: **These topics might be discussed in order to get a different perspective of the lives most of us lead in our society. Take each of the five questions seriously.**

1. What would happen if professional and college coaches were not paid according to their won-loss records?

2. What would happen if fat people really were regarded as highly as thin people (as is true in some countries)?

3. What would happen if we could only have names that are on a list of approved first names published by the government (which is true in Sweden)?

4. What would happen if the manufacture of gas guzzling vehicles was strictly prohibited?

5. What if <u>you</u> were never arrested for breaking the law?

You can choose the one or two questions that you think are most provocative for your students, or you can devise a couple of your own.

Reference

Torrance, E. P. and H. T. Safter. <u>Making the Creative Leap Beyond</u>. Buffalo, N.Y.: Creative Education Foundation Press.

"INSIDE"

There are two ways in which we can **visualize internally**. One is to try to imagine what is inside an object, a problem, or a concept. The other is to commune with oneself, to meditate, to probe one's being. We have the student do both in this lesson.

Thinking skills emphasized

- **visualizing things internally**
- being original
- analyzing
- making judgments
- hypothesizing

Torrance (1999) asserts that all of the creative problem solving models recognize the importance of finding hidden facts and elements in the problem so that they can be dealt with. Highly creative individuals are able to go beyond externals and visualize the internal workings of things.

Activity Taking a Look at the Feelings and Motives Inherent in an Argument Between Two Close Friends (30-35 minutes)
Activity Sheet "Look Inside Yourself"

Introducing the Activity

Since this activity is a highly personal one, you should mention that your students are to tackle it individually and that the activity sheet isn't to be turned in. "Look Inside Yourself" requires a good deal of contemplation and so should be undertaken when the student is somewhat tranquil and has an opportunity to be meditative. The activity itself won't take a half-hour if your students don't take it seriously and don't answer the questions honestly.

Administering the Activity

Other than giving your students enough time and the security of knowing that their responses are strictly private, you don't have much to do for this activity. It will be time well spent, however, if your students take it seriously. For the ones who don't spend much time introspecting, use "Following Through" activities.

Following Through

There are probably several productive activities that can follow "Look Inside Yourself." Among them might be:

• On their own, your students can look for examples in literature of problems similar to theirs.

• Each student can write a song, play, poem, or story about this experiences.

• Each student can create a design or draw a picture that is inspired by his experiences.

• Each student can compile some tips for resolving an argument.

Notes

LOOK INSIDE YOURSELF

When was the last time you had an argument with a close friend?

What was it all about? What was the central problem?

What did it mean to you?

Is it resolved now?

Was it a matter of your pride or ego? If so, in what way?

Was it a matter of a simple misunderstanding? If so, what was the misunderstanding?

What shouldn't have been said?

What should have been said?

Describe your feelings during the argument.

Describe your feelings after the argument.

Describe your feelings now.

Draw a diagram of the forces within you at the time of the argument. What forces were in conflict? Show them in your diagram.

If you had a conversation with yourself about the argument, what would it be like?

What conclusions can you draw about the argument?

Extensions

Activity Imagining Objects and Places Rarely Seen and Then Finding Out About Them (45-50 minutes in class)
Activity Sheet "What's Inside?"

Introducing the Activity

There is a fascinating game called "What's in the Box?" that teachers have long used to sharpen the investigating skills of their students. Something similar can be used by you to put your students in the mood for this activity. Just find a box or some container about the size of a lunch box and place one object or several of the same kind (for example, rice, raisins, or beebees) inside. Have your students take turns going to the box and asking a question after doing whatever they want with the box (except opening it up). Note the students who smell the box or listen intently to the sounds which come from rattling it. As a guessing game, this activity is fun, but it can also be revealing with regard to how your students pick up clues and reason.

Administering the Activity

After a discussion of objects and places we are familiar with but rarely see the inside of, seven commonplace places and objects are named for speculation concerning their interiors. We ask that your students imagine what the inside of a substation, fire house, or hornet's nest looks like. There may be students who actually know from their own experience, but since it is unlikely that any student will have knowledge of the interiors of all seven objects, this activity's objective, namely, to stimulate the student's imagination and reasoning powers, will likely be reached.

We suggest that, after imagining what the seven objects or places are like inside, your students actually try to find out. We wonder how often students are invited inside the teachers' lounge.

Following Through

Among the activities that might follow the administration of "What's Inside" are these:

• A fruit such as an orange, apple, kiwi, or fig can be sliced in half. There are pleasing patterns to be found when you look at the fruit in this way. Even though it is such a common thing to do, you can get a few surprises from examining the fruit very carefully.

• You can say: **There are places that are not meant to be viewed from the inside. What places are they? Why aren't most people able to view them?** A list of such places can be made up after some research is done. This is best accomplished by groups of three or four students.

• You might challenge your students with: **What's inside a church steeple? After finding out for sure, draw a picture of the inside of a church steeple.**

• You might say: **What's really at the center of the earth? There are several theories about it, but does anyone know for sure?** The students can do some research about this question either individually or in groups.

Activity Listening for Clues and Hidden Meanings in Little Stories
Activity Sheet "What's the Hidden Meaning?"

You can present this activity to sharpen your students' sensitivities to the hidden elements in situations and problems so that the real problems can be identified. By giving the little stories to them orally, rather than in written form, you will give your students practice in listening for details and sifting information.

Reference

Torrance, E. P. and H. T. Safter (1999). <u>Making the Creative Leap Beyond</u>. Buffalo, N.Y.: Creative Education Foundation Press.

Notes

WHAT'S INSIDE?

1. Farmers and people who live in the country see those cylindrical structures known as silos, and they know exactly what to expect if they were to look into one. That holds true for grain elevators also. Similarly, people who have been around trains a good deal are familiar with what is inside a caboose, but most of us only see a caboose from the outside, bringing up the rear of a long freight train. There are probably many things you know very well from the outside and not at all from the inside. But you probably have your ideas about what they are like inside.

Here are various items that we see fairly often, but we usually know little about them internally. Although you may never have been in them, describe what you would expect to find if you were able to inspect them from the inside. Give as full a description as your imagination permits.

a. a substation for generating electricity

_____

_____

_____

_____

b. a fire house

_____

_____

_____

_____

c. what is under a manhole cover in the street

_____

_____

_____

_____

d. the vault in a bank

_____

_____

_____

_____

e. a hornet's nest

_____

_____

_____

_____

f. the rear end compartment of a VW bug

_____

_____

_____

_____

g. the teachers' lounge at school

_____

_____

_____

_____

2. If you receive an invitation, look into any or all of the seven places named above.* See if your ideas about what is inside them are correct.

*Although it's unlikely that the hornets will invite you inside.

WHAT'S THE HIDDEN MEANING?

1. Mrs. Jordan hadn't seen her friend Mrs. Cooper for several years because she had moved away from Brownsville. When she visited Mrs. Cooper and her twelve-year-old son Bobby one afternoon, she remarked: "It's really good seeing you again, Marva. And Bobby. He's certainly improved since I saw him last."

   What is the hidden meaning in Mrs. Jordan's words?

   _____

   _____

   Why do you think so?

   _____

2. A boy gets a haircut only a week after his last one. When his father asks him why so many visits to the barber, he says: "Oh, I thought I looked a little shaggy." The boy has just turned fifteen.

   What's the hidden meaning in the boy's getting another haircut?

   _____

   _____

   Why do you think so?

   _____

3. A girl gives her most precious locket to her next-to-best friend. Her best friend has always admired it greatly. The girl and her best friend haven't quarreled, but they like all the same things.

   What is the hidden meaning of the girl's giving the locket?

   _____

   _____

   What makes you think so?

4. Jasper was a fairly conscientious worker, and he had expected to be promoted quickly in his job as warehouseman for a large manufacturing firm. He watched unhappily as Tim, Abdul, and James were promoted ahead of him in a matter of 18 months. Jasper was afraid to complain to Clancy, his supervisor.

One day they happened to be taking a break at the same time. Clancy smiled at Jasper and said: "Keep up the good work, Jasper. We need men like you who can be depended on to always show up every day."

What was the hidden meaning in Clancy's words?

_____

_____

What makes you think so?

_____

_____

5. Although his teammates weren't sure why, Nestor got to play a full quarter of every game as defensive back on the football team. He wasn't fast, and he didn't tackle very well, but he got into the game anyway. Maybe the best things that could be said about his football playing were that he practiced hard and listened eagerly to the coach. He also asked the coach intelligent questions.

When Nestor's father asked him how a practice had gone, Nestor said: "Oh, pretty well, Dad."

"I'm sure you did your best, Nestor. And Coach Miller will notice that. I've always thought he was a good guy, ever since we roomed together in college."

What was the hidden meaning in Nestor's father's words, although he may not have realized it himself?

_____

_____

Why do you think so?

_____

LESSON 16

"PUSHING THE LIMITS"

Of Torrance's 18 creative thinking skills, **extending boundaries** calls for the most of an individual's resources. It is the skill that you must call upon when combining, synthesizing, seeing in different perspectives, producing alternatives, visualizing richly, and the rest aren't enough to gain a successful solution to the problem. Your students will not easily seize and develop this skill.

Torrance (1999, p. 218) has named his sixteenth creative thinking skill **extending boundaries**. He defines it as looking outside a problem situation, redefining or reworking the problem situation to find a question that, if answered successfully, would set in motion changes leading to the creative solution. He uses the familiar nine-dot problem as a way of exemplifying this skill.

•　•　•

•　•　•　　　　Connect all nine dots in straight lines without

•　•　•　　　　lifting your pencil.

Until you go outside the immediate area of the nine dots, you can't solve the problem. Typically, we restrict ourselves to only the area encompassed by the dots and this self-imposed restriction makes it impossible to solve the problem.

Thinking skills emphasized

- **extending boundaries**
- orienting to the future
- being original
- analyzing
- making judgments
- hypothesizing

Activity Delving into the Idea That Some Kinds of Hoarding Are Justifiable and Some are Not and Projecting the Implications of Future Hoarding (2 class periods)
Activity Sheet "More Than Enough"

Administering the Activity

If the student hasn't confronted it in the initiating activity, we are forcing him or her to examine the notion that hoarding is justifiable in certain situations. The very controversial – and important – part of this question is whether it is all right for a nation to stockpile nuclear weapons. You may or may not want to have your students investigate this issue.

Your students are only asked to consider how much or how little hoarding they might be doing in 10 years. They are not to write a formal essay. Of course their situations will be much different a decade from now. Many of them will be self-supporting. Whereas an eleven-year-old boy might engage in possessing as many baseball cards as he can get hold of, at 21 he's more likely be interested in accumulating money. He'll be the rare individual if at that age he can hoard much money, but there may be items he will be acquiring faster than he can use.

If none of your students believe she will be doing any hoarding at all 10 years from now, press them on the matter. Each of us has some one thing that we have acquired too much of to make use of in the near future. It is likely that 10 years from now the acquisitive instinct will be fairly strong in most of your students, too.

Following Through

You might very well follow up "More Than Enough" with these activities:

• A discussion of hoarding is necessary in order that your students be able to sort out their ideas and clarify them. The issues raised by this activity are complex and deep. It may be that some students will have definite ideas about "storing for future need" and saving for possible emergencies.

• Any list of future shortages necessarily entails some predicting or guessing of a high order, but a look at present shortages can give us strong clues of what the shortages in the future might be. Therefore, have your students look rather thoroughly into our present problems of habitable space, atmospheric pollution, scarcity of water and energy, and the others.

Of the many follow-through activities that might be engendered by "More Than Enough," these are a few that could be suitable:

• Conduct a general discussion of the problem and the students' solutions.

• In case there is some controversy during the discussion, a formal debate can take place. The regular rules of debate can be observed.

• Volunteers can role play a situation featuring the hoarding of gasoline, water, or some kind of food. Select a commodity that is currently in short supply and high demand.

• Investigate the cause of a shortage that is currently impacting the community.

• Begin a unit of study about the crisis or near-crisis being caused by a shortage somewhere in the world.

MORE THAN ENOUGH

1. If you could have more than you will need for the next year, what would you store up or save?

Water? Why or why not?

_____

_____

Firewood? Why or why not?

_____

_____

Salt? Why or why not?

_____

_____

Sugar? Why or why not?

_____

_____

Toilet paper? Why or why not?

_____

_____

Chewing gum? Why or why not?

_____

_____

Soap? Why or why not?

_____

_____

Coffee? Why or why not?

_____

_____

Flour? Why or why not?

_____

_____

Canned fruit? Why or why not?

_____

_____

For various reasons, all of these things have been saved by people from time to time. When a human being or an animal stores up more of something than could possibly be used in the near future, we call this activity <u>hoarding</u>. Crows, squirrels, and pack rats are some of the better known hoarders of the animal kingdom. During times of famine, pestilence, and war people are liable to hoard food or oil or anything that is in short supply.

It is understandable for people at times to get more than their normal needs require. During World War II people tried to obtain as much as possible of certain items that were mostly going to the armed forces. Those items were rationed by the government. A system was worked out whereby each citizen was entitled to buy a limited amount of these items, based on his or her needs. Generally speaking, the system worked well. Recently, nations have been hoarding oil, gold, grain, and nuclear missiles.

2. Are <u>you</u> justified in hoarding anything right now? _____ If so, what? _____

Why are you justified in hoarding it?

Is our country hoarding anything now? What is it hoarding?

_____

_____

Explain why it is all right – or wrong – for the country to do this hoarding.

_____

_____

What is the most important question to ask about this hoarding?

_____

_____

3. In 10 years what will you be hoarding and why will you be hoarding it?

_____

_____

_____

_____

_____

_____

_____

_____

_____

_____

_____

_____

Developing the Concept of Hoarding

At the beginning of the activity the student is presented with the idea of hoarding (acquiring more than is needed). We deepen the student's understanding of the concept by asking if he or she would hoard any of 10 items that people have hoarded and are still hoarding. It may seem ridiculous to a youngster who lives near a lake for anyone to hoard water, but there are many people in arid regions who desperately want to store as much water as they can. Similarly, most young people aren't too interested in storing a lot of salt, but a large percentage of the world's population is concerned about having enough salt in the future.

Not too many years ago there was a paper shortage in Japan, and nearly every Japanese tourist came home from North America with an extra supply of toilet paper. Controlling the number of diamonds that are sold throughout the world is the legitimate business of powerful firms, and they often accumulate an over-supply of diamonds in reaction to market conditions. People are hoarding all kinds of things now, including everything on the list.

And yet the word hoard generally connotes an activity that is dishonorable, disagreeable, and/or sinful. Perhaps a student's attitude about a particular case of hoarding will be determined by the reasons for the hoarding. If the individual, company, or nation hoards because of avarice or ambition, the student is not so likely to feel good about the activity. If the person, corporation, or country hoards in order to survive, the student is likely to look with more favor at the hoarding. How your students react to the idea of the excessive storing up of salt, firewood, soap, coffee, and the other items should be illuminating. Recognizing the socio-psychological reasons for hoarding any of the 10 things will contribute to a better understanding of why people behave as they do.

Extensions

Activity Discussing the Plight of a Fisherman Who Can't Catch Enough Fish to Make a Living (45-50 minutes) **Activity Sheet** "Fished Out"

Preparing for the Activity

Discussion of changing occupations, migrations of people, conservation and endangered species, and natural resources can all lead in nicely to the administration of this activity. In all likelihood, one of those topics has been dealt with in class, and all you have to do in warming up your students is to refer to it.

Administering the Activity

Allow your students to muse about Mona and her father on their own. If you have dealt with this kind of problem in class, your students should be able to think deeply about the issues it raises for all of us, even though we may not have a family member who is directly affected. (Incidentally, the biggest single occupation at risk in the United States is farming.)

Perhaps the key question is: If the fisherman has found that the poor catches he has experienced mean that he can't support his family, why does he keep on fishing?

Following Through

Activities that could naturally follow "Fished Out" include:

• Discuss the predicament of the fisherman in depth. If it is harder and harder for commercial fishermen to earn a living fishing, why do these people continue to rely upon it for their livelihood?

• Are fishermen having this trouble in other areas of the country (New England, Gulf Coast, Pacific Northwest, and others)? Through the Internet and periodicals, do some intensive research about fish populations in the Atlantic, Pacific, and the Gulf of Mexico.

• What other occupations are less and less able to support their workers? Conduct a survey of "endangered" occupations. At a minimum, have your students make a list of the jobs that are dying out in this country. The Occupational Outlook Handbook is one government publication that could help.

• Write a report on a "fading" occupation. There are excellent films featuring people still engaged in occupations such as blacksmithing, weaving, bookbinding (by hand), and others that would tie in nicely with this important topic. Either show one of these films for the class, or permit each student to choose the occupation for her report.

• Have your students look up the word "perseveration."

FISHED OUT

Mona's father is a fisherman. He has been a fisherman since before Mona was born. For the past three years Mona's father hasn't caught many fish. There have been very few fish in the sea to catch.

After the poor catch last season, Mona's mother asked her husband to find another job. He said, "Fishing is the only thing I know how to do." So he fished this season, and the catch was even worse.

Mona doesn't want to move to another town, but all of the fishermen in her town are becoming very poor. They say that the fishing is going to be poor next year, too. If they moved, Mona would miss her friends in the third grade, but she knows her mother is right. Her father should find another job.

What suggestion do you have for Mona and her family? If there is a poor catch again next year, they will lose the house they have been buying. What should they do?

_____

_____

_____

_____

_____

_____

_____

_____

_____

_____

_____

Activity Investigating the Reasons for Migrations of People
(45-50 minutes)
Activity Sheet "Moving"

Introducing the Activity

Americans must be a very restless group of people. We move a lot. Therefore, this activity should be meaningful to many of your students. By simply asking ("raise your hands") which class members have moved in the last five years, you'll be able to lead in to the activity in an effective way.

Administering the Activity

The statements and questions leading up to the final question are designed to get your students thinking rather deeply about why people move from place to place. The second set of questions is meant to be challenging (how could these events result in a migration of people?). If you can think of others that are more provocative, please substitute them.

The migrations of animals and people are really fascinating, and we must assume that in every case there are reasons for the migrations.

Following Through

You can follow up "Moving" with one or more of these activities:

• Ask for anecdotes from class members concerning their own moves.

• Write a narrative of "My Most Memorable Move."

• Show a film about planned cities.

• Investigate the concept of urban growth boundaries.

• Do research on the Internet and in periodicals concerning recently displaced peoples in Africa.

MOVING

It is said that the average family in the United States moves every three years. If your family is "average," then you've gone to more than one school. Moving, in a way, is scary; but it's also exciting and challenging.

When animals move from one area to another, they have a definite reason for doing so. People do, too, but they have many more reasons for changing their residences. What are some of the reasons that people move from one town or city to another?

If you have moved from one city or town to another one, what was the main reason for your move?

We might compare the migrations of birds, whales, lemmings, reindeer, and salmon to those of people. People move for some of the same reasons.

1. What kinds of people regularly move to places where there is more food?

_____

2. What kinds of people migrate regularly to a warmer climate each winter?

_____

3. Are there people who return to the same location to give birth to and/or raise their children? If so, describe them.

_____

Keeping in mind that a migration, generally speaking, involves a large number of individuals, tell why these events might result in a migration.

1. a bank robbery

_____

_____

2. a drought

_____

_____

3. the construction of a school

_____

_____

4. a baseball game

_____

_____

5. a war

_____

_____

6. the election of a president

_____

_____

7. a flood

_____

_____

8. knocking down the trees of an orchard to build houses

_____

_____

9. a wedding

_____

_____

What major changes in our society and on earth might make us less restless and not inclined to move often at all? Think about global as well as national conditions and events that might make moving a rare event.

Alternate Activity Solving the Problem of a Cluttered Room (45-50 minutes)
Activity Sheet "Enough Already!"

Introducing the Activity

You can introduce this activity with only a remark or two about the universal problem that parents have in persuading their offspring to keep their rooms neat. You might ask: **"How do you feel about keeping your room neat? Is it important to you? Is it important to your parent(s)?**

One or more of your students may say, "What's the big deal, anyway?" and you'll have a good lead-in to "Enough Already!"

Administering the Activity

This activity can be administered to the group as a whole, or individual students can mull over the issue on their own. If you have students work on it independently, you can have a discussion when they have written adequate responses on their papers.

The problem of keeping a daughter's or son's room half-way neat is an ever-present and universal one. Encourage your students to give it some serious thought. One or two may break through and extend the boundaries of the problem.

Following Through

Activities that can follow the completion of "Enough Already!" include:

• Have your students role play a confrontation between a parent and a son or daughter about keeping a clean room. You can use Mervin and his mother or take a situation suggested by one or more of your students.

• Have your students finish the story about Mervin and his mother in writing.

• Have your students finish the story and illustrate it.

• Some – perhaps a majority – of your students may share a room. What complications does sharing a room have for a young person? Have the students who share a room tell about the problems.

Reference

Torrance, E. P. and H. T. Safter (1999). Making the Creative Leap Beyond. Buffalo, N.Y.: Creative Education Press.

ENOUGH ALREADY!

Mervin's mother thought that there was a big problem in the way he was keeping his room. It was badly cluttered, and the biggest source of the clutter was Mervin's magazines. He had been acquiring all kinds of magazines, but he didn't throw them out after they were old. He collected sports magazines and hot rod magazines and outdoor magazines and much more. Mervin just kept them in piles, in a more or less organized fashion.

On several occasions Mervin's mother had suggested that the excess, the amount over that which could be neatly stored on shelves, be taken to the dump inasmuch as the local recycling company didn't accept slick magazines. To her it was a simple matter of Mervin's not being able to read all of those magazines, especially since he continues to acquire more. So far, he has resisted his mother's attempts to get rid of the extra magazines.

Is there any other way of looking at this problem? Can you see any way out of Mervin's dilemma? To find a solution, you will have to look at the problem in a different way than either Mervin or his mother does.

_____

_____

_____

_____

_____

_____

_____

_____

_____

_____

_____

_____

"WHAT'S FUNNY?"

The central and pervading creative thinking skill featured in this lesson is letting **humor** flow. Humor is hard to analyze, but it isn't hard to recognize when our funny bone is tickled – then we are liable to laugh.

Thinking skills emphasized

• **letting humor flow**
• being original
• analyzing

Walker (1992), states that of all the acts of which human beings are capable, laughing is probably the most essential to survival and sanity. Researchers have long tried to establish a connection between an individual's having a sense of humor and her being creative. According to Torrance (1999), humor and laughter are basically creative and are facilitative of the creative process. He offers these clues for the teacher in identifying creative students in the classroom:

• portrays the comical, funny, amusing in role playing;

• portrays the comical, funny, amusing in drawings;

• makes humorous, original comic scripts;

• makes people laugh a lot in games;

• makes up humorous jokes or stories;

• makes people laugh (not make fun of) in discussion;

• describes personal experiences with humor;

• plays jokes on others.

Activity Playing a Punning Game with Adverbs and Prepositional Phrases (45-50 minutes)
Activity Sheet "Briefly"

Introducing the Activity

This lesson encourages your students to take an in-depth look at that basic – some say base – form of humor known as the pun. (If you yourself don't like puns, this lesson probably won't be very successful.) Depending upon your purposes, this unit can lighten up a somber class or provide an opportunity for your students to gain some insights about humor.

Administering the Activity

Since the pun is meant to be humorous, the activity should be administered in a light-hearted manner. When humor is analyzed seriously, it often turns out to be a mystery as to what it was that was thought to be so funny. That's the danger in taking this activity too seriously – when your students look hard at the puns they will find that they won't be convulsed.

Nevertheless we can encourage them to be discriminating in their preferences for the many kinds of humor they are exposed to, especially on television and in films.

When introducing "Briefly" to your class, you might say something like this: **This is a game that will stretch your minds a little. If you are good at punning, it won't be hard. But even if you have a little trouble, keep at it – a word will come to you.**

In this lesson, your students are to work independently. It should be entertaining to have them try out their "brieflies" on their classmates.

Here are some possible answers to the six questions in "Briefly":

1. Jerry won the match <u>handily</u>.

2. Herbert finished <u>barely</u>.

3. Ellen's experience of going through the maze without a mistake was <u>amazing</u>.

4. Doug is regarded <u>highly</u>.

5. The congregation received the minister's word <u>as gospel</u>.

6. The tightrope walker performed <u>with airs</u> or <u>loftily</u>.

A sharp student may realize that <u>all</u> of the answers to the questions aren't adverbs or prepositional phrases. "Amazing" is certainly an adjective, but it wasn't tossed out because it is in the spirit of the game (and a fairly good pun).

Following Through

If time permits, one or two of the following activities might prove worthwhile in following up "Briefly."

• Have your students complete a survey of their newspapers and decide whether the pun is overused.

• Invite your students to make a "secret" survey of the use of puns at school, recording the frequency with which puns are used by teachers, aides, secretaries, administrators, custodians, volunteers, and other students in a 24-hour period.

• Have your students compose jingles or jump-rope rhymes that contain puns.

• Those students who are talented at expressing themselves in drawing can draw a cartoon whose caption contains a pun. This could be a collaborative effort among two or more students – one or more to compose the pun and one to draw the cartoon.

• If there are students who dislike puns, ask them to analyze the reasons.

• Your students could compose additional "brieflies," and in so doing they can develop their skills of cooperation, leadership, and tact.

Reference

Myers, R.E. (2002) <u>Word Play: Language Lessons for Creative Learners.</u> Marion IL: Pieces of Learning.

Notes

BRIEFLY

A. Sometimes all you need in order to respond to a question is one or two words. The usual short answers to a question are "Yes" and "No," but in some cases you can use an adverb or prepositional phrase to adequately express your response. For example, if a blind man purchases an article in a store and is given a nickel in change instead of a quarter, how should he react? "Feelingly" (an adverb) or "with feeling" (a prepositional phrase) might be good answers.

   Come up with short answers to questions such as the one above. Each answer you give should be a pun. What would you say in these situations?

1. Jerry is a skilled boxer who is exceptionally quick with his hands. A brash young newcomer challenged Jerry to a fight one day in the gym. How did Jerry win?

_____

2. Herbert joined about a hundred swimmers in a race across the channel, but half-way across he lost his trunks. How did he finish?

_____

3. The first time Ellen saw a maze in an English garden, she got through it without a mistake. How would you describe Ellen's experience?

_____

4. Doug was nearly seven feet tall. He was an honest, hard-working electrician who often replaced light bulbs in ceilings without a ladder. How did people regard Doug?

_____

5. The minister's sermon was gripping, and the entire congregation hung on his every word because it was based on an important lesson in the Bible. In what way was the minister's service received?

_____

6. The stuck-up tightrope walker thought he was above everyone in the circus, both literally and figuratively. How did he perform his act?

_____

B. Create questions with similar one- or two-word answers in the form of adverbs and prepositional phrases. Write at least three.

Extension

As a follow-up to "Briefly" you can assign "Mighty Punny." There is hardly a day that I don't see a punny headline in the local newspaper, and I'm sure that your newspaper has just as many writers who are terribly fond of puns. Puns seem to be irresistible to them.

Activity Finding Punny Headlines in the Newspaper (homework)
Activity Sheet "Mighty Punny"

Notes

MIGHTY PUNNY

1. When Imelda Marcos, famous for having hundreds of pairs of shoes, decided to run for president of the Philippines, this letter was sent to an editor of a West Coast newspaper under the heading, "Well-heeled candidate:"

"If Imelda Marcos runs for president of the Philippines, she should be a shoe-in."

This is an example of someone using that beloved – and hated – device, the pun. The newspaper added a pun of its own in the heading because Mrs. Marcos is also a very wealthy widow.

According to Webster, a pun is "a play on words of the same sound but different meanings or on different applications of a word, for the witty effect." It is one of our oldest and most overused forms of humor. Hardly a day goes by that most newspapers don't use several puns, often in the headlines and headings of stories and features. Sports pages are a rich source of puns. For example, on consecutive days one newspaper had these headlines:

"Oilers defense too slick for Jets in clutch." (Houston Oilers versus New York Jets in professional football)

"Blazers struggle to cut down the Nets." (Portland Trailblazers versus New Jersey Nets) Basketball fans catch the pun easily because they know that cutting the nets is what literally happens by the victorious team in a championship game.

A pun that came naturally to the copy editor of a large West Coast newspaper was "Martinez Pitcher Perfect." Dennis Martinez of the Montreal Expos team had pitched nine innings and had not allowed a batter to reach first base – a "perfect game." The headline is a pun, of course, because of our expression, "picture perfect." The basis for many puns is a similarity in the sounds of words, as stated in the first part of the definition; and the words can also be identical and have two meanings, as in the "well-heeled" example.

2. Find a newspaper or magazine and see if you can find some puns. Write at least four.

3. Now find three stories, in any of the many sections of the newspaper, and write punny headlines for them. First write three or four sentences summarizing the story, and then write a headline with a pun about it.

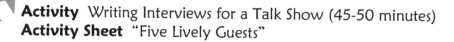

Activity Writing Interviews for a Talk Show (45-50 minutes)
Activity Sheet "Five Lively Guests"

If you would prefer to get away from puns (they do wear you down after awhile), this is an approach to humor of a different kind. "Five Lively Guests" features bizarre characters in a talk show, but there is an emphasis upon language again because your students are to dream up an interview with each of those most unusual guests. This will give you an opportunity to teach the skills necessary for writing direct quotes.

To lead into the activity, you might say: **Do you like talk shows on television or radio?** (Wait for responses.) **Well, I know some people who love them and a few who hate them. I have an activity here that features five screwball guests on a talk show. I think you might enjoy them.**

Preparing for the Activity

This activity invites the student to write an interview. Its inspiration is the exchanges between the host of a radio talk show, whose role is to be assumed by the student, and "five lively guests." The guests are described in the opening section of the unit.

The unit can serve as a reason for introducing the skills involved in writing dialogue, or it can be a review of those skills. If you would like to prepare your students for this unit with an exercise concerning quotations, here is one that will help them distinguish between direct quotations and indirect quotations.

Murray's Antics

Place quotation marks around those words in the following story that are direct quotations; that is, the exact words of a speaker as he or she speaks them. Do not put quotation marks around indirect quotations, those words that represent approximately what a person said.

Murray, according to his classmates, was a kooky and undependable young man. Jerry, the boy in class who was kindest to him, called him several uncomplimentary things, but Jerry actually liked Murray. He did it again! Laura groaned. What did who do? asked Jerry. Murray! He snatched my pencil when I wasn't looking. Oh, that. What's a pencil to you? You've got plenty of pencils, said Jerry. But then he tried to balance it on his forehead and it fell to the floor, and Miss Conklin asked whose pencil it was. Laura then frowned and related how Murray had told Miss Conklin what a lovely girl she was and how she had such a sweet disposition.

In going over the exercise with your class, you can point out that the traditional way of handling dialogue is to put one speaker's words in a separate paragraph. If they do it that way, there will be seven paragraphs in all. None of the direct quotations are broken. You can save that skill for another time.

Administering the Activity

In common with many talk shows, this imaginary one imposes a time limitation on the host in asking questions. Only three questions can be asked of each of the five guests. The guests are most unusual for a talk show: a tea bag collector, the elderly winner of "The World's Prettiest Toenails" contest, a modern day Diogenes, a cockroach trainer, and a young woman who is an expert at recognizing cars.

The student is to write, in direct quotations, the exchanges with one of the unusual guests. Accordingly, she or he must know the difference between a direct and an indirect quotation. The unit's last sentence tells the student that in a direct quotation the words of a speaker are given exactly as they are spoken (and are enclosed in quotation marks). This unit thus reinforces the writing skills needed in writing dialogue, even as it challenges the student's imagination in coming up with dialogue that should be both interesting and colorful.

Evaluating the Activity

You can use the exercise suggested above and the unit itself as a pre- and post-test of the skills needed to write dialogue. When your students write their interviews, it will be apparent if they are indenting and using quotation marks correctly. On the other hand, you may not want to evaluate their work formally, preferring to reward their imaginative thinking in dreaming up their interviews.

Following Through

A natural follow through activity for "Five Lively Guests" is a discussion of television and radio talk shows. You can see the danger inherent in opening up such a discussion, Your students will engage in a haphazard gabfest about their favorite and unfavorite personalities. Nevertheless, you might be able to help your students to develop some criteria for informative talk shows.

References

Torrance, E. P. and H. T. Safter (1999). Making the Creative Leap Beyond. Buffalo, N.Y.: Creative Education Foundation Press.

Walker, B. R. (1992). Laughing Together. Minneapolis, MN: Free Spirit Publishing.

FIVE LIVELY GUESTS

Let's suppose that you are the host of a radio talk show. Your show features unusual people as guests, and you also have people phone in and express their opinions. Next week you have a great show lined up for Tuesday. These will be your guests:

1. A dapper accountant from Okmulgee, Oklahoma, who has saved every tea bag he has used for the past 27 years. A great tea drinker, he drinks all brands but never touches instant.

2. The 61-year-old winner of the World's Prettiest Toenails Contest, a grandmother from Fairbanks, Alaska.

3. A man who, after 15 years of non-stop searching, has succeeded in finding an adult who has genuinely liked all of the presidents who have held office during his lifetime. The contented citizen, who has never voted in a national election, refused to travel to the studio for an interview. He doesn't like nosy people.

4. A woman who trains cockroaches to do tricks. She started out to have a flea circus, but soon discovered she was allergic to fleas. She also found out that silverfish are impossible to train.

5. A young woman who can tell at a glance the difference between an Accord and a Lumina a half-block off. She also can distinguish a '57 Volkswagen beetle from a '58 beetle (but at close range).

Because of time limitation, you will only be able to ask three questions of each guest. What would be the three questions that would bring forth the liveliest responses from:

The Tea Bag Collector

1. _____

2. _____

3. _____

"Grandma Toenails"

1. _____

2. _____

3. _____

The Modern-Day Diogenes

1. _____

2. _____

3. _____

The Cockroach Trainer

1. _____

2. _____

3. _____

The Car Expert

1. _____

2. _____

3. _____

You plan to write the exchanges between you and one or two of your guests after the program. (You'll have an audio tape made of the program.) They will be included in a newsletter that the network sends out to loyal listeners of your program.

Select one of your interviews and write it as if you were submitting it to the person who puts together the materials that go into the newsletter. Use your imagination in guessing how that guest will respond to your three questions. Be sure to use quotation and punctuation marks in the proper places. The interview will consist almost entirely of direct quotations. In a direct quotation, the words of the speaker are given exactly as s/he spoke them.

"TO THE FUTURE"

In this lesson, your students are invited to do some predicting and serious thinking about their futures. Most of us enjoy predicting the scores of a game or what some person will do next. Addicted gamblers will even bet about the color of the next car turning the corner. The kind of predicting to be done in the activities to follow, however, is of the "informed guess" variety. With sufficient knowledge to back our predictions, we can hope that we'll have good guides for our actions.

Thinking skills emphasized

- **orienting to the future**
- being original
- being sensitive, finding the problem
- being aware of emotions
- analyzing
- making judgments
- hypothesizing

In the past three decades there has been a tremendous interest in thinking about the future. Educators have taken the study of the future seriously, especially in the wake of the furor caused by Alvin Toffler's books in the seventies. One of the leading proponents of having young people think about the issues facing society and humanity is E. Paul Torrance, co-founder of the Future Problem Solving Program, which involves over 250,000 students each year in all 50 states and several foreign nations. In these competitions, students write scenarios about the important problems that we must solve in the future. Evidently putting themselves in hypothetical situations that require solutions to real problems is quite beneficial to the young people who participate, developing their intellects in ways that can't be realized in reviewing, analyzing, and evaluating the past (Crabbe, 1991).

Torrance (1999) believes that not only is the ability to **orient to the future** necessary in achieving one's goals, but that an individual's image of the future is a better predictor of future achievement than is her past behavior. A number of applications of this theory can be found in What Next? (Myers and Torrance, 2001).

Activity Interpreting Six Scenes and Making Predictions about Events That Could Take Place on the Following Day
(3 class periods and 3 days)
Activity Sheet "And You Are Invited"

Preparing for the Activity

Although timing and time are factors in every classroom activity, this is the kind of activity that can be administered at almost any time. The "gimmick" in the activity is that your students are supposed to put themselves into the situations that are prescribed. So they are supposed to do something (in their imaginations) as a result of receiving those sense experiences (saw, then heard, then smelled; saw, felt, heard; and the like). An anecdote about how someone behaved when confronted with a challenging set of circumstances would be an excellent way to introduce the activity. Unfortunately, there are plenty of occasions when people are faced with threatening circumstances in hurricanes, floods, earthquakes, and other natural disasters. You may well know of a good story that will set the stage for "And You Are Invited."

Administering the Activity

"And You Are Invited" starts off with six scenes, each featuring three different sense experiences, which your students are to interpret. After telling what might be going on, they are to commit themselves to a course of action because they are to imagine that they are in the scene they are witnessing.

At the second level of involvement, your students are asked to make predictions about a variety of events that could take place on the following day. Then they are to record (on the next day) what actually happened. Finally, they are to make up their own set of questions about future events that interest them and then predict what will happen. Keeping score about how accurate their predictions turn out to be might intrigue even the most blasé of students.

This activity takes more than three days. Your students are to respond to the initial section on the first day and make predictions about events on the following day. Then they are to keep a record of how well they did with their own predictions of favorite events in the near future.

How you will handle the second and third levels will be determined by how much time you want to devote to these activities. You may only want to use the first-level activity as a springboard for creative writing. It can prove to be a productive session for simply inducing your students to write something (anything!). On the other hand, I believe that your students will enjoy the prediction activities as well. One of the most fascinating aspects of life is trying to figure out what will happen next. Without that ever-present question about the future, life would be worse than drab.

Following Through

If your students turn out to be budding futurists, you might look into some of the excellent materials available from the Future Problem Solving Program. In particular, two of their publications, Research Challenges and the Scenario Writing Guide might prove very useful.

AND YOU ARE INVITED

1. How quick-witted are you? Can you size up a situation quickly and then take appropriate action (or not at all if it is best not to do anything)? How would you interpret the following situations?

a. What would you suppose might be going on if . . .

you stepped from your house and heard a great deal of howling and saw hundreds and hundreds of cats and smelled a very pungent odor?

_____

_____

_____

What would you do?

_____

_____

_____

b. What do you suppose might be happening if . . .

you were on a boat and heard a roar and saw strange flashes in the sky and felt a strong breeze?

_____

_____

_____

What is your next move (if any)?

_____

_____

_____

c. What would you think might be going on if . . .

you entered your classroom and smelled a strong acid-like odor and heard foreign-sounding music and saw no one in the room?

_____

_____

_____

What would you do?

_____

_____

_____

d. What do you suppose could be happening if . . .

you were sleeping in a tent near a stream and felt dampness on your arm and smelledsomething very sweet and heard two guttural grunts and then couldn't open your eyes?

_____

_____

_____

What would you do?

_____

_____

_____

e. What would you think might be going on if . . .

you drove into town in a car and saw people running excitedly up the street toward you and heard <u>no</u> shots or sirens and smelled nothing unusual?

_____

_____

_____

What would you do then?

_____

_____

_____

f. What do you suppose might be happening if you approached your house one evening and heard coughing, a grunt, a hysterical laugh, and a chuckle inside?

_____

_____

_____

Would you go in? Why or why not?

_____

_____

_____

180

2. Most of the events in our lives come as no surprise. We expect things to happen in a certain way, and, for the most part, they do. However, it is the unexpected which gives life excitement, humor, and zest. If we could predict every event, life would be drab and almost pointless. But don't take our word for it – why don't you find out for yourself? Do a little predicting and discover whether most events can be predicted (but may come as a shock or mild surprise).

What will your mother say to you when you first see her tomorrow morning?

Your guess: _____

What really happened: _____

_____

When you wash your hands and face, will the water from the faucet be hot right away or will it take a little time to warm up?

Your guess: _____

What really happened: _____

_____

How much traffic will you see on the road or street which takes you to school?

Your guess: _____

What really happened: _____

_____

Will you see any animals on your way to school? If so, what kinds?

Your guess: _____

What really happened: _____

_____

Will the trees or bushes have changed color or lost any of their leaves?

Your guess: _____

What really happened: _____

_____

What will your teacher say first thing in the morning when school begins?

Your guess: _____

What really happened: _____

_____

What will be the first thing you have to do when the class starts?

Your guess: _____

What really happened: _____

_____

Who will be the first one to ask the teacher a question?

Your guess: _____

What really happened: _____

_____

Who will be the first one to go up to the teacher after class has begun?

Your guess: _____

What really happened: _____

_____

What will happen at lunch?

Your guess: _____

What really happened: _____

_____

What is the first thing you will do when school is over?

Your guess: _____

What really happened: _____

_____

3. Were your predictions fairly accurate? Were you far "off base" on any of your guesses? How do you account for being wrong?

_____

_____

4. What would life be like if things rarely happened the way we had anticipated?

_____

_____

_____

_____

_____

_____

5. Make up your own set of questions about school, sports, social events, changes in nature, news events, or anything else that particularly interests you. Make your predictions and then keep a record of how well you foresaw the future.

Extension

Activity Listening for Details (given orally)
Activity Sheet "Three Quickies"

An entertaining and instructional activity that might follow "And You Are Invited" is this listening exercise. Read these three, or three other, brief stories. Your students are to listen for details so that they can guess what the scenes are all about. Each scene has a key missing fact omitted, and the behavior of the characters is perplexing.

Notes

THREE QUICKIES

Down by the Riverside

A blind girl went down to the river at the edge of town in order to listen to the river. When she arrived at the river bank, she heard some water splashing. Bending down to touch the ground, she knocked a pebble over the side of the bank. In a few seconds, she stepped back. The color had drained from her face. Why?

One of Those Nights

Jerry Martin rushed into the house at the sound of the second clap of thunder. His mother and sister were putting the supper dishes away as he passed through the kitchen. He gave his mother a nervous glance. She did not look worried, but his sister Mary did.

When the flash of light lit up the living room five minutes later, Jerry grunted and clapped his book shut. A little gasp escaped from his mother. Everybody hesitated, and then started moving. Mary and Mrs. Martin quickly grabbed some objects off the dining room table.

"Owww!" cried Mary. "That wax burned my fingers!"

At just about the same moment Mr. Martin barked his shins against the staircase. "Brother!" he grumbled. "Let's get to bed."

What had happened? What was the reason for the Martins acting as they did?

Don't Get Pushy!

Two boys were sauntering along a sidewalk one day on their way home from school. One of the boys, a short, stocky fellow, shuffled along, giving half of his attention to a robin pecking in a nearby lawn and half to his companion's chatter. The other boy, a tall, freckle-faced youngster, was talking about what it must be like to be a rich lawyer. Suddenly, the taller boy shoved the stocky boy to one side and fell to his hands and knees.

Why did he behave that way?

Activity Predicting What the Student's Life Will Be Like When He or She is 30 Years Old (45-50 minutes) **Activity Sheet** "Your 30th"

Preparing for the Activity

Some remarks by you regarding birthday celebrations or just events lying in wait in the future would lead nicely into the administration of this activity. Young people don't have much conception of what being 30 years old is. Older people have always laughed at them because youngsters in adolescence think of 30 as being quite old. That is one reason that the 30th birthday was chosen for this activity.

Administering the Activity

The first section is a long list of questions concerning where the student will be on her 30th birthday. Please add to or delete questions from the list as you see fit. Technology has changed so much in the last couple of generations that it is hard to imagine exactly how anyone will live 15-20 years from now where communications and entertainment are concerned. If you have a good question in those areas, include it.

The next section must be completed at your student's home because it calls for her to look for 10 items that she hopes will be in her home on that fateful 30th birthday. Finally, we ask your student to touch those 10 items and then say whether they will feel the same on her 30th birthday.

Following Through

Among the activities that could follow "Your 30th" are these:

• Talk to two people who are 30. Ask them whether things are different from how they were when they were your age. Also ask them how they are different from how they imagined things to be when they were your age.

• Talk to two people who are 60. Ask them why it is better to be 30 and also why is it better to be 60. Do they think you'll be better off than they are when you are 60?

• Draw a picture of your principal means of transportation on your 30th birthday.

• Describe your favorite food when you are 30.

• Name and draw a picture of America's favorite breed of dog when you are 30.

References

Crabbe, A. B. (March/April 1991) Future Problem Solving. Gifted Child Today, 14 (2), 22-24.
Myers, R. E. and E. P. Torrance (2001). What Next? Waco, TX: Prufrock Press.
Torrance, E. P. and H. T. Safter (1999). Making the Creative Leap Beyond. Buffalo, N.Y.: Creative Education Foundation Press.

YOUR 30TH

1. How will you spend your 30th birthday? In some ways that birthday will be like your others, but in many other ways it will be different. Where do you think you will be on your 30th birthday?

In what part of the world will you be?

_____

If you are in this country, in what part of the country will you be?

_____

Will you be married?

_____

If there is a party, where will it be held?

_____

At what time of day will it take place?

_____

And if the party is away from your home, how will you get there?

_____

Will there be any entertainment?

_____

And, if so, what kind will it be?

_____

What will you be wearing?

_____

What kinds of gifts will you be happy to receive?

_____

What kinds of food will be served?

_____

How long will your birthday party last?

_____

At the end of the day, where will you sleep? _____

2. When you go home, look around carefully. What items will you still have in your own home on your 30th birthday? Name at least 10 that you hope very much will be there.

1. _____

2. _____

3. _____

4. _____

5. _____

6. _____

7. _____

8. _____

9. _____

10. _____

If you can, touch each of those ten things. Will every one of them last? Will they feel much different when you are 30?

_____

_____

_____

_____

_____

_____

_____